S0-AFS-151

Learn everything from beginning-to-advanced features of your operating system, applications, and peripherals to finance management and personal development. Learn to surf the Internet, e-mail digital photographs, and edit digital video, as well as how to set up a home network and manage your finances. You can sharpen your office software skills and even learn to build a web site. Plus, you have 13 months from the date of purchase to access the courses.

To purchase, go to
LearnDell.com/completepc

$10.00 OFF
Complete PC
Training Package

at LearnDell.com/completepc

GUIDE TO

PC
Fundamentals

Ultimate Guide for New Computer Users

Discover

the potential

of your new

computer

LearnDell.com

Faithe Wempen

To Margaret, for the usual reasons.

Acknowledgments

Thanks to the wonderful Course Technology PTR editorial staff for another job well done.

About the Author

Faithe Wempen, M.A., is an adjunct instructor of Computer Information Technology at Indiana University/Purdue University at Indianapolis, specializing in PC hardware architecture, Windows, and business applications. Her 13-plus year career in the IT industry has included experience as a PC repair technician, computer book editor, teacher/trainer, and freelance writer, and she has written more than 90 books and hundreds of Web and magazine articles.

Faithe is the author of the college textbook *PC Maintenance: Preparing for A+ Certification* (EMC/Paradigm) and retail books on PC tune-up, upgrade, and certification, including *A+ Jump Start* (Sybex), *A+ Fast Pass* (Sybex), and *Tune Up Your PC in a Weekend* (Premier Press). Her recent software titles have included *Windows XP Home Edition Simply Visual* (Sybex), *The PowerPoint 2003 Bible* (Wiley), and *PowerPoint Advanced Presentation Techniques* (Wiley).

Faithe is a contributing editor at CertCities.com, where she reviews CompTIA A+ and Microsoft Office exams and provides tips for helping PC repair technicians become more successful. She is on the advisory panel for the PC Technician training program at Training, Inc. of Indianapolis, and writes and teaches courses in Advanced Windows XP, PC Maintenance, and Microsoft Office online for clients, including Hewlett-Packard, eMachines, and Netscape.

Contents at a Glance

Contents

Part II
Common Computing Tasks 87

12 Upgrading Your PC **223**

Introduction

Welcome to *PC Fundamentals*! In this book you will find all the information you need to get started with your new computer—or to make the most out of an existing one.

This book is for people who are new to computing, or who feel like they have missed out on the basics somewhere along the way. It offers a gentle introduction into many of the most popular computing topics today, including the Internet, multimedia, digital imaging, and even upgrading and troubleshooting. This book is easy and fun to read and eases you into the technical terms and concepts you need to know to use a computer with confidence.

This book is divided into three parts:

Part I: "Setting Up and Customizing Your PC." You'll start with the basics here, learning how to choose the right computer for your needs and how to set it up yourself when you get it home. (No need for expensive professional installation!) If you're brand new to the Windows operating system, you will appreciate the no-experience-required Windows tutorial in this section. This part also shows you how you can customize many of the settings on your PC to make it work more naturally and comfortably for you and how you can install and remove application software such as word processors, spreadsheets, checkbook programs, and games.

Part II: "Common Computing Tasks." In this part you will learn about many of the useful things your computer can do for you, including connecting you to the Internet (and securing your privacy and security there), capturing pictures with a scanner or camera and then printing them out on a printer, and organizing collections of music and video clips.

Part III: "System Maintenance." This part will help you keep your computer in good working order. It shows you how to clean and maintain a computer and provides some tips for troubleshooting when things go wrong. In this part of the book you will also learn how to set up a home network and how to make smart decisions about upgrades.

Throughout this book you'll find clear, readable text and attractive graphics. Where special information is available, it will be pointed out in the following boxes:

Definition: Important vocabulary words.

TIP

Suggestions for improving your productivity or making features easier to use.

NOTE

Background information or extra options relating to the topic being described.

CAUTION

Possible hazards or pitfalls to be aware of.

I hope you enjoy this book and that you will find it a useful first step in your journey into computer proficiency.

PART I

Setting Up and Customizing Your PC

1

Choosing and Setting Up a Computer

In this chapter:

- ◆ Basic PC anatomy
- ◆ Shopping strategies
- ◆ Unpacking and connecting a new PC

Welcome! Whether you've just purchased your first computer or you're considering one, this chapter will help you get started on your journey toward PC mastery. You'll become familiar with some of the most common technical terms and specifications, and you'll find out how to make smart shopping decisions and set up a new computer for use.

Basic PC Anatomy

PC stands for personal computer—a computer designed to be used by one person at a time. PCs were a big deal when they first appeared back in the 1980s because up until that point most computers were huge, expensive, and designed for large businesses. Some people use the term PC to refer only to personal computers that run the Microsoft® family of operating systems (such as Microsoft Windows® XP) and make a distinction between PCs and computers that run other operating systems, such as the Apple Macintosh operating system.

The physical parts of a PC are known as *hardware,* and the programming instructions that a PC executes are *software.* The following sections look at the most important types of each.

Hardware: Physical computer equipment such as drives, circuit board, cases, and chips.

Software: Instructions that tell the hardware what to do.

System Unit

The most important piece of hardware is the *system unit*—the big box into which everything else connects. Inside the system unit are the electronics that make the computer do its stuff.

On the front of the system unit are panels and slots for accessing disk drives (such as CD and floppy). The front usually also has a power button and one or more indicator lights. See Figure 1.1. On the back of the system unit are *ports* for connecting external devices such as a monitor, a keyboard, a mouse, and so on.

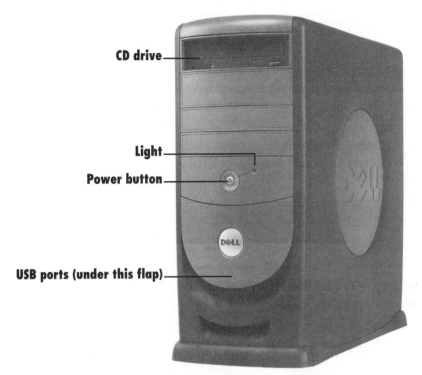

CD drive

Light

Power button

USB ports (under this flap)

FIGURE 1.1 The front of a typical PC.

You don't have to know what's inside the system unit box to use a PC any more than you need to know how to pop the hood on a car to drive. But when you're shopping for a new PC, the inner parts are what makes one PC cost more than another, so it's a good idea to know what's going on in there. Here's a peek:

✦ **Central Processing Unit (CPU).** A microchip that serves as the "brain" of the computer, processing most of the mathematical operations that make it function.

✦ **Random Access Memory (RAM).** A set of microchips that work together to create a temporary holding area for data as the computer is operating.

✦ **Motherboard.** A big circuit board that serves as a central gathering point. The RAM and CPU are mounted on it, and most of the other inside components connect to it, also.

◆ **Hard Disk.** A sealed set of metal platters for storing data. The hard disk typically is the primary storage device.

◆ **Other disk drives.** Most systems have at least one CD drive, and it might also have DVD playing capability, and/or the ability to write to CDs and DVDs. There might also be a floppy disk drive.

◆ **Power Supply.** Computer components require low voltage (+2 to +12 volts) direct current (DC), such as a battery provides. Household outlets provide high voltage (110v) alternating current (AC). The PC's power supply bridges the divide by stepping down the incoming voltage and converting DC to AC.

Figure 1.2 shows the inside of a computer. Don't be intimidated by that nest of cables and connectors—it isn't critical that you understand what every little wire is for, any more than you would need to know every hose and pipe under your car's hood in order to drive it.

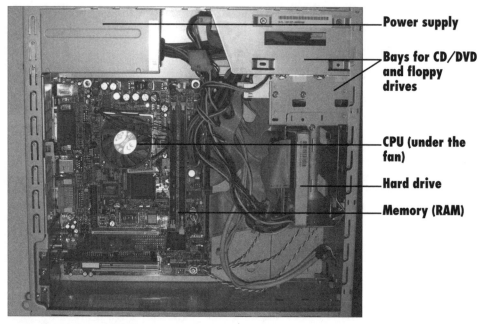

FIGURE 1.2 Inside a typical PC

Input and Output Devices

The system unit is the central gathering point for the *input* and *output devices*.

The most common input devices are the keyboard and the mouse. As you type or click, you input data and instructions to the computer. Another fairly common input device is a digital camera, which inputs pictures.

The monitor is the most essential output device—without a monitor, you have no way of knowing what your computer is doing! In addition, printers output data files, and speakers output sound and music.

Input device: A device that helps you get data into the computer.

Output device: A device that displays data that's coming out of the computer.

Communication Devices

Some devices exist to help the PC communicate with other PCs. They enable two-way communication, so they are both input and output devices.

You will need a communication device in order to connect to the Internet (see Chapter 5, "Getting Started with the Internet"). If you will connect via a dial-up connection, you'll need a *modem*. If you will connect in some other way, you will need specialized equipment for your chosen connection method (for example, a terminal adapter box for a DSL or cable connection or a satellite dish and transmitter/receiver box for a satellite connection). When you sign up for Internet service, the company you pick to provide your service can advise you as to the needed equipment and in many cases can even sell it to you (or give it to you for free!).

Modem: Short for *modulator-demodulator*. A device that translates digital data from a computer into audio signals for transmission over phone lines and then back again at the other end.

If you plan on networking your computers together in your home or small business, you will also need a network interface card (NIC) for each computer. Chapter 10, "Setting Up a Home Network," explains home networking and details the equipment you will need for it.

Storage Devices

Storage devices are another gray area in the input/output realm. They take in data from the computer's memory and hold onto it, so in that sense they are output devices. But later they are able to reload the stored data back into the computer's memory, so in that sense they are input devices. Storage devices include floppy disks, hard disks, CDs, DVDs, tape backup units, and flash RAM devices.

There are several ways of classifying storage devices:

◆ **Disk versus non-disk.** Some storage devices are *disks*, and some take other forms, such as magnetic tape (like a cassette tape, only wider).

Disk: A flat circular platter that spins on a central axis and stores data on its surface.

◆ **Removability.** Floppy disks, CDs, and magnetic tapes can be removed from their *drives*, so you can play multiple disks with a single drive. Hard disks are permanently joined to their drives, such that the terms "hard disk" and "hard drive" are roughly synonymous.

Drive: A mechanical unit that reads and writes data on a disk or on magnetic tape. It typically includes a motor that drives the spindle that turns the disk, a read/write head on a movable arm, and a disk intake and ejection system.

◆ **Storage technology.** Some disks store data magnetically (hard disks, floppy disks, tape drives), and some store it optically (CDs and DVDs). The difference is in the method used to read and write the disk. Magnetic drives use magnets and magnetic sensors, while optical disks use lasers and light sensors.

Software

The purpose of storage in a computer is to hold software. Unlike hardware, which you can see and touch, software does not exist in a physical sense. Software is like knowledge. It can be stored and transferred using physical objects, but it is not a physical object itself.

There are two main types of software you can buy in stores:

◆ **Operating system.** This software starts up your PC and keeps it running. It enables you to manage your data files and communicate with input and output devices. Microsoft Windows XP (see Figure 1.3) is the most popular operating system today.

◆ **Application.** This software works with the operating system to enable you to do something useful, such as write a letter or balance a checkbook. Examples include word processors, spreadsheets (such as in Figure 1.4), databases, and games.

In addition, there is a third type of software: data files. When you save your work in an application, it creates a data file and puts your work into it. You specify a name and location for that file on a disk, and then later when you want to work with that same data again, you reopen that file.

FIGURE 1.3 Microsoft Windows XP is the most popular operating system.

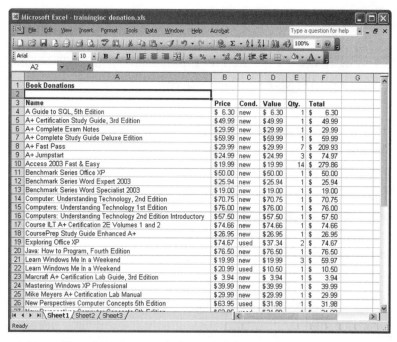

FIGURE 1.4 Microsoft Excel is a popular business application.

How to Shop for a Computer

Now you know about the main parts that make up a computer, both hardware and software, but so far I haven't given you any specifications or recommendations. That was on purpose—I wanted you to get a feel for the computer in a generic sense before piling all that on your plate.

So now let's assume you're going to shop for a PC. There are many models available, each with a huge array of choices. How do you sort it all out?

One easy way is to get some free professional help from a Dell representative. Just call 1-800-915-DELL (that's 800-915-3355) and a knowledgeable salesperson will ask you about your needs and budget and recommend a computer that will fit.

Another way is to explore the Dell Web site at http://www.dell.com and browse for notebooks or desktops. But wait—which of those do you want?

Notebook or Desktop?

The first consideration is whether you want a notebook or a desktop PC, because you'll be shopping in a whole different part of the store (or Web site) depending on your answer.

A desktop PC is an ordinary PC, the kind with the big box (as in Figure 1.1) and separate monitor. The main benefit of a desktop PC is price. Desktop PCs are inexpensive. You get more for your money with a desktop PC than with a notebook in terms of power, speed, and storage space.

Desktop PCs also have a few other benefits, which may or may not be of interest to you:

◆ **Ease of servicing.** Desktop PCs tend to be built from industry-standard parts, so that if a part were to fail after the warranty had expired, you might be able to buy a replacement at your local computer store and install it yourself (or with a little help from a techie friend). Notebook PCs, on the other hand, tend to use parts made specifically for that brand, so if your notebook PC fails after it is out of warranty, you'll probably need to take it to a repair shop. Of course, for most people this is not a big deal since they would not want to work on their own PCs anyway!

◆ **Expandability.** A desktop PC's case is much larger than a notebook's (obviously) and contains expansion slots for adding new devices such as drives and circuit boards. Notebook computers are less expandable simply because there's less extra room. It is possible to add many capabilities to notebook PCs using PC card devices and external USB devices, but if you are planning for major expansion, such as adding a second hard drive, a desktop PC might be a better choice.

In contrast, notebook PCs are more portable. They typically have a built-in monitor and a built-in keyboard and pointing device (which replaces a traditional mouse). The main draw, as you probably guessed, is *freedom*. With a notebook computer, you aren't tied to a desk—or even an electrical cord. Just pack up your computer and go. Figure 1.5 shows a typical notebook PC.

NOTE

You might think it would be a drawback to have a notebook PC if you spend most of your time at a desk, because of its smaller monitor and keyboard. However, you can connect an external monitor, keyboard, and mouse to a notebook PC so that it becomes an "engine" that can drive a complete desktop computing system.

FIGURE 1.5 A typical notebook PC.

Which Line of PCs?

Let's assume you're going to buy a Dell. (This is a Dell book, after all!) Dell makes a lot of different models, and not all are appropriate for home and small office use. Some are high-end workstations for sophisticated applications such as Computer-Aided Design (CAD), and some are servers for running large networks. You'll run into this with whichever PC brand you go with, not just Dell. No one model is ideal for every purpose.

The most popular Dell lines are:

✦ **Dimension.** Desktop PCs suitable for general home and office use.

✦ **Inspiron.** Notebook PCs suitable for general home and office use.

✦ **Optiplex.** Desktop PCs optimized for use on large corporate networks.

✦ **Latitude.** Notebook PCs optimized for use on large corporate networks.

✦ **Precision.** High-end workstations (desktop or notebook).

✦ **PowerEdge.** Network servers.

For home and small office use, Dimension is the right choice for a desktop and Inspiron for a notebook. Anyone who is buying a computer for any other use is probably an experienced computer professional who would not need this book.

So let's assume you've decided to look for a Dimension desktop at the Dell Web site, in the Home & Home Office area of the site. Some important choices still need to be made, because Dimension desktops come in several different models.

The model numbers change periodically, but you can rank them by the first digit of the model number. As the first digit goes up, so do the price and the features. For example:

- ◆ Dimension 2400: Entry-level value mode.
- ◆ Dimension 4600: Mid-level, a good balance of price and features.
- ◆ Dimension 8300: High-end and powerful, with the latest technology.

Each of these models has a default configuration, but can be fully customized during the ordering process. So that brings up our next question.

Which Features?

One way to shop for a PC is to simply accept the default configuration. There's nothing wrong with that. But personally, if I'm going to spend the money for a new PC, I want it to be customized to my exact specifications.

After selecting a model from the Dell Web site, you can click the Customize It link and then select from a list of dozens of customization options. I'll describe some of the most popular ones in the following sections.

CPU

The central processing unit (CPU) is the microchip that takes in raw data, performs math operations on that data, and spits it back out again. It's the "brain" of the computer, and the faster the brain works, the faster the computer itself operates.

NOTE

Physically, the CPU is a very small and thin wafer of silicon mounted on a ceramic chip. (The ceramic part channels heat away from it.) That ceramic chip is then either mounted on the motherboard or mounted on a small circuit board that in turn fits into a slot in the motherboard. See Figure 1.6.

FIGURE 1.6 A typical CPU (courtesy of Intel Corporation).

The CPU is a difficult piece to upgrade later because many other components are designed around it. Therefore, your first decision should be which CPU you want: brand, model, and speed.

CPU speed is measured in gigahertz (GHz). Most CPUs in new PCs sold today run at between 2.4GHz and 3.5GHz, although by the time you read this, there will probably be even faster ones. Faster is better, but faster also costs more. The fastest CPUs are usually available for desktop PCs, with notebooks lagging behind by six months or so, because it is more difficult and costly to make a smaller, cooler-running CPU.

CPU speed is such a moving target that the best way to shop is to figure out "how much am I willing to spend to have the fastest CPU available?" There will likely be a several-hundred-dollar price difference between the computers with the fastest and the slowest CPUs in the store. I have found that the best values are usually in the middle to bottom range.

NOTE

When you pay more money for a faster CPU, what you are really buying is *time*. You are staving off the purchase of your *next* computer, several years from now, by a few months or maybe even a year. No matter how fast the computer you buy today is, in about three years it is going to seem really slow because the technology advances so quickly. When you go shopping for new software a few years from now and you're reading the box to determine the minimum system requirements, will your computer squeak by or be inadequate? If you spring for the faster CPU now, you buy yourself a little extra time where your computer will continue to squeak by.

Here are some of the popular CPUs you might be able to choose from as you customize your order:

◆ **Intel Pentium 4 Processor:** A solid-performing CPU for desktop and notebook PCs running mainstream applications for business and pleasure.

◆ **Intel Pentium 4 Processor with Hyper-Threading Technology:** A more feature-rich and efficient version of the above, suitable for use in both general and high-end systems.

◆ **Intel Pentium M Processor:** A CPU designed specifically for notebook computers, helping them to have longer battery life (among other benefits). When judging the speeds of CPUs, you can't compare this CPU one-to-one with others because it performs just as well at lower speeds as desktop PC CPUs do at higher ones. For example, a 1.6GHz Pentium M is equivalent to a 2.4GHz Pentium 4.

◆ **Intel Centrino:** A combination of the Pentium M processor (above) with a special motherboard chipset and a wireless networking adapter.

◆ **Intel Celeron:** An economical CPU for home and small business computers that will be used primarily for simple business applications and the Internet.

RAM

Random access memory (RAM) creates the temporary work area that the computer relies on as it runs. Having enough random access memory (RAM) is very important in making the computer run fast, not just in how much you can do at once.

NOTE

Physically, RAM is a little circuit board mounted on the motherboard. The most common type is a dual inline memory module, like the one shown in Figure 1.7.

FIGURE 1.7 RAM modules like these provide the temporary storage in your PC.

Microsoft Windows requires a lot of RAM to work well, and if a system runs out of memory, all kinds of trouble can result, ranging from lockups to programs refusing to start. Therefore, Windows has a built-in overflow system called *virtual memory*. Whenever the PC runs out of RAM, it automatically uses part of the hard disk as a temporary holding area to swap data into and out of the real RAM so that Windows doesn't completely run out of available RAM. This allows Windows to keep running no matter how much you try to do at once, but there's a drawback—swapping data in and out of RAM from the hard disk is time consuming, and it makes the computer run slower than normal. The end result is that a computer that doesn't have enough RAM will tend to run much more slowly than one with plenty of RAM if you are using it to perform complex or multiple tasks.

There are different speeds and types of RAM, but that decision is made by your choice of PC model. Each model of PC has a certain kind it uses (for example, Dual Channel DDR SDRAM is one type).

How much RAM is enough? Again, this is a moving target because RAM requirements are constantly escalating. A few years ago, 32 megabytes (MB) was considered ample. These days, 256 megabytes (MB) is the minimum amount to consider in a new PC. If you are going to play the latest 3D games on your PC or use it for photo manipulation or 3D graphics creation, or if you typically have a half-dozen applications all open and running at once, you may find it beneficial to go with a larger amount of RAM, such as 512MB or even 1024MB.

Hard Disk Space

The next consideration is disk space. Most PCs come with hard disks of anywhere from 40 to 160 gigabytes (GB). How much do you need? That depends on what you're going to be doing with the PC. If you are just going to be word processing and using the Internet, then a smaller hard disk of 40 GB should be just fine. However, if you have a large collection of music and video files, or you have a lot of games or business applications that all need to be installed, go for the largest hard disk you can afford.

Depending on the model, you may also have a choice of hard disk technology. The hard disk industry is in a state of transition to a new standard called Serial ATA that uses a new type of cable to connect the hard disk to the motherboard. If possible, choose Serial ATA over the older standard (Ultra ATA/100).

CD and DVD Drives

Most desktop PCs can accommodate at least two CD or DVD drives in the case, and you can always hook up external drives via the USB port later if needed. A typical PC these days comes with one or more of these drive types:

- ✦ **Standard CD-ROM Drive.** This is the least expensive option. It plays CDs but not DVDs, and it does not write to either CDs or DVDs.
- ✦ **Writeable CD (CD-RW).** This type of drive reads CDs and writes to CD-R (write-once) and CD-RW (write multiple times) discs.
- ✦ **DVD.** This type of drive reads both CDs and DVDs but does not write to either.
- ✦ **DVD-R or DVD+R.** This type of drive reads both CDs and DVDs and writes to both. There are two standards for writeable DVDs: DVD+R and DVD-R. You may see a drive advertised as DVD±R, which means it does both.
- ✦ **DVD/CD-RW Combo.** This type of drive does everything a standard DVD drive does, plus it writes to CDs (but not DVDs).
- ✦ **DVD±R/CD-RW Combo.** This drive does it all: It plays both CDs and DVDs and writes to both CDs and DVDs.

You can choose between a single drive and dual drives. Dual drives are handy when you want to copy a disc, but you can still copy discs with a single drive—you just copy the data from the disc to your hard drive temporarily and then onto the writeable disc.

Floppy Drives

Fewer and fewer PCs these days come with floppy drives, simply because people don't use floppy drives much anymore. Applications all come on CD, so there is little reason to use a floppy.

If you don't think you will need a floppy drive, look for a model without one and save a few bucks. You can always get an external floppy drive later if you decide you need one. There are also many other ways of transferring files, such as digital media readers, writeable CDs or DVDs, and flash memory devices.

Which Display?

The display is an important consideration in choosing a PC because it's the primary output device through which the PC communicates. There are two parts to the video display: the video card inside the PC and the monitor that you hook up to it.

Video Support

The computer talks to the monitor by way of a video adapter. The video adapter has a particular make and model that is separate from the PC itself. People who are very interested in PC gaming will have strong opinions about which video adapter is the best, but for general use any will probably be fine.

Some economy model desktop PCs—and all notebook PCs—have the video adapter built into the motherboard. On mid-level and high-end desktops, the video adapter is a separate circuit board inside the PC. All other things being equal, having it on a separate circuit board is better because it makes it easier to upgrade.

Video RAM is also an issue. The video adapter requires a certain amount of RAM to operate. The exact amount depends on the display resolution you are using. If the system has a separate video board, it will have some video RAM installed on it. However, if the system has built-in video support, it probably draws the RAM it needs from the general RAM pool for the system at large.

Having shared video RAM is not necessarily a bad thing as long as you have an adequate amount of RAM in the system in general. The video adapter can use up to 32MB or even 64MB of RAM, so you want to make sure that you get enough RAM in the system that if 32MB or 64MB of it were subtracted, you would still have more than enough to do what you want to do. Because of this possibility, I recommend that you get at least 512MB of regular system RAM on systems with shared video RAM.

If you are getting a high-end LCD monitor (discussed in the next section), you will want the video card to support DVI (Digital Video Input), a special type of connector for hooking up a digital monitor. LCD monitors can be used with regular video cards, but the quality is better if they use the DVI connector instead.

Monitor

Two monitor technologies are available today:

- ◆ **CRT.** Stands for cathode ray tube. This is the traditional "box" kind of monitor that has been used ever since PCs were first developed. They are bulky and heavy, but cheap. See Figure 1.8.

- ◆ **LCD.** Stands for liquid crystal display. This is the flat kind of monitor, shown in Figure 1.9. They are thin and lightweight and produce beautiful images. However, they are more expensive than CRTs, especially for large sizes.

FIGURE 1.8 CRT monitors are large and heavy but economical.

FIGURE 1.9 LCD monitors are lightweight and take up very little space.

Screen size is one way that monitors differ. Screen sizes are measured diagonally, and common sizes are 17", 19", and 21".

TIP

You may see CRT screen sizes described as two different numbers, such as 16.1"/17" or 16.1 viewable. That's because the original measurement method for screen sizes included the portion of the monitor glass that was hidden behind the monitor's plastic bezel. No fair, huh? You were paying for screen space that you weren't able to see! The smaller number (16.1", for example) is the actual viewable screen size. This makes a difference when comparing two monitors. For example, two 17" monitors might have actual viewable sizes of 15.7" and 16.3"; the latter one would give a half inch more viewable screen, even though they are both marketed as 17" monitors.

Refresh rate is another measurement of a CRT monitor's capability. Inside a CRT is an electron gun that refreshes the illumination of each dot on the screen many times per second. The faster it can do this, the less your monitor flickers, so a higher refresh rate is better. When comparing refresh rates between two monitors, you have to compare them at the same screen resolution. For example, if one monitor supports 75Hz refresh at 1024×768 and another one supports 120Hz refresh at 800×600 resolution, that's not a fair comparison, and you can't extrapolate any meaningful data from that. On the other hand, if those refresh rates were both for 1024×768, the one with the higher rate would be better. On an LCD monitor, typical refresh rates are lower; a good-quality LCD might have a vertical scan refresh of 60-75Hz, for example.

Finally, dot pitch is an issue for CRT monitors. This refers to the distance between the individual phosphorescent dots (pixels) that comprise the monitor screen. A lower number is better (the dots are closer together). A typical CRT monitor might have a dot pitch of .243 mm, for example. This is called *pixel pitch* on an LCD monitor.

Other Hardware

We're almost done! Here are just a couple of other considerations when selecting a PC.

Networking

If you have more than one PC in your home, consider networking them. It's really very easy, especially if all the PCs have the same version of Windows (preferably Windows XP).

There are two kinds of networking: wired and wireless. Wired is the traditional type. If your PC comes with a network adapter card (NIC) that advertises itself as 10/100BaseT Ethernet, that's a wired one. If it describes itself as 802.11b or 802.11g, that's wireless.

I don't want to turn this into a chapter on networking (that's Chapter 10), but I do want you to be at least somewhat aware of this networking stuff now because there's no point in paying extra for a PC with a wired network adapter if you know that two weeks after you get it you are going to set up a wireless network.

> **NOTE**
>
> Gigabit Ethernet is a faster, newer networking standard, and not necessary for a home or small office. If you are buying a PC to work on a corporate network, ask your network administrator whether you could benefit from upgrading to a Gigabit Ethernet adapter.

Modem

If you still connect to the Internet via dial-up through a phone line, you will need a modem in your new PC. You can remove the modem from the old PC and install it in the new one (usually—it depends on whether Windows XP drivers are available for it), but you may find it more convenient to simply shop for a PC that comes with a modem.

Sound Support

1

Most systems these days come with basic sound support, including ports for plugging in speakers and a microphone. If you just want to listen to the occasional audio CD and play some games, whatever the PC comes with should be fine. On the other hand, a high-end sound card is an inexpensive upgrade, so why not treat yourself?

If you are a more serious audiophile, consider shopping for a PC with a high-end sound card. (If you're that serious about music you probably already are aware of what's available! Creative.com is the best-known company that produces them; they make the SoundBlaster line.)

If you are a musician with an electronic keyboard, you will probably want to hook up your keyboard to your PC. You can do this with a *MIDI* interface. The sound card may support this directly, or you may need to buy a USB-based MIDI interface at a local music store or computer store.

MIDI: Musical instrument digital interface; an interface for connecting electronic musical instruments to a computer.

If video editing and music mixing is important to you, make sure you get a sound card that supports those activities. Some sound cards have built-in compression systems that make it easy to watch, convert, and edit movies.

Speakers are priced separately from the sound card, in case you already have speakers you want to reuse. The amount to spend on speakers depends on how much you plan on using the PC as a media center, for playing music and DVDs. If you want great quality, go with the high-end speaker sets.

Software

One nice thing about buying a new computer: You generally get a lot of free software with it. The packages vary, but with all new computers you get at least the following:

   ◆ The latest version of the Microsoft Windows operating system

   ◆ Software for connecting to the Internet and using the Web and e-mail

   ◆ A desktop application suite such as Microsoft Works, Microsoft Office®, or Corel WordPerfect Office

Do you need Windows XP Home Edition or Windows XP Professional? It all depends on how you plan to use the PC. If you will not be connecting to a large corporate network and do not require the highest levels of security, then the Home Edition is probably fine for you. However, be aware that you cannot connect a Home Edition computer to a domain-based network (such as in a large company). Home Edition works fine with simple peer-to-peer networking of up to 10 computers.

In addition, most systems come with limited trial versions of other software, such as programs for listening to music clips, checking for viruses, or editing graphics.

If you need more software than what comes with your chosen PC, you'll need to set aside some money in your budget. As you are preparing your plan, go shopping for software and find out how much it will cost to get what you want. Some software you may want to consider budgeting for:

◆ Home publishing packages that enable you to make posters, greeting cards, and other printed projects.

◆ Games for children (or adults!).

◆ Software for importing and editing still graphics or video clips.

◆ Programs that help you manage your home finances or fill out your income tax forms.

Unpacking and Connecting a New PC

Okay, so you've made your decision, bought the computer, and now it's sitting in a big box in the middle of your office or living room. And you're fighting two conflicting impulses: 1) to rip everything open like a kid on Christmas morning, and 2) to put off opening it for as long as possible because you have no idea how to assemble it.

Let's put that fear to rest, because Dell computers are extremely easy to set up and come with clear, well-illustrated instructions (in color, even!).

Here are the basic steps for new computer assembly:

1. Take everything out of the boxes and remove all plastic wrap, packing, twist-ties, and so on. Make sure you got everything you paid for.

2. Place the monitor in the desired location. Sit in a chair in front of it, and make sure it's a good height and angle for you.

③ Place the keyboard in the desired location. Again, sit in front of it and practice typing a bit. Your forearms should be parallel to the floor. If they're not, the keyboard is at the wrong height, and it's going to make your wrists hurt.

④ Place the mouse in the desired location and try it out. Your forearm should be parallel to the floor, and your hand should come straight out of your arm, not tilted to the left or right.

⑤ Scout around for the best place to put the system unit. You will need to be able to reach its CD and floppy drives easily, and the cords for the monitor, keyboard, and mouse will all need to be able to reach to the back of it.

⑥ Plug the monitor into the back of the system unit. This is not that difficult because the monitor fits in only one place (the 15-hole D-shaped plug). See Figure 1.10. If your motherboard has built-in video support, the VGA plug will be up higher, mixed in with the other ports (shown in Figure 1.11).

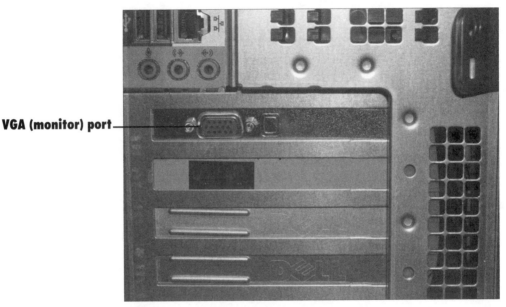

VGA (monitor) port

FIGURE 1.10 A VGA monitor connector on the back of a PC.

NOTE

If you have a high-end LCD monitor, with a DVI (Digital Video Input) connector on it, you can connect it to the DVI port on your video card if it has one. This is optional (you're free to use the VGA port instead), but it results in better video performance.

---

⑦ Look at the ends of the cords to your keyboard and mouse. If they have round plugs (called PS/2 style), look for corresponding round holes on the back of the system unit, as shown in Figure 1.11. There will be two: one labeled with a little picture of a keyboard, and the other with a picture of a mouse. They may be color coded as well. If the plug on either the keyboard or the mouse is a flat rectangle instead, that's a USB connector, and it plugs into a USB port. Most computers have these on both the front and back. Figure 1.11 shows them on the back.

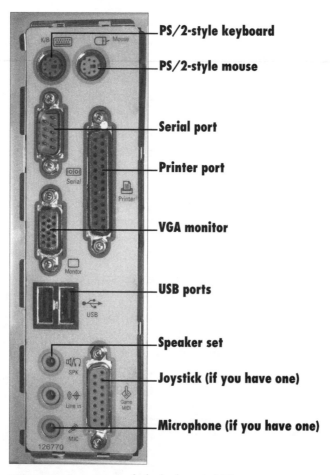

PS/2-style keyboard

PS/2-style mouse

Serial port

Printer port

VGA monitor

USB ports

Speaker set

Joystick (if you have one)

Microphone (if you have one)

FIGURE 1.11 Connectors on the back of a typical PC

⑧ Plug the monitor's power cord into the monitor and into a grounded wall outlet or power strip.

⑨ Plug the system unit's power cord into the system unit and into a grounded wall outlet or power strip.

⑩ If your PC came with speakers, connect them as shown in the diagram that came with them. Speakers plug into the green or black plug on a sound card; in Figure 1.11 sound is built into the motherboard so the speakers would connect to the middle (green) round connector.

NOTE

Perhaps you are wondering how you can get stereo sound out of a single connection to the sound card. On simple two-speaker systems, one speaker connects to the PC and the other one connects to the first speaker. On bigger-and-better speaker systems, a sub-woofer connects to the PC and all the other speakers connect to it.

⑪ Turn the monitor on. Look for an amber light to illuminate on it and perhaps a test message to appear on its screen.

⑫ Take a deep breath and turn the computer on. The light on the monitor will turn green, and you'll start seeing messages on the screen as the computer boots (that is, starts up).

The first time you start your new computer, you will be guided step-by-step through a setup and registration process. Just follow the prompts.

When it's all over and your computer is working well, pack up all those empty plastic bags and twist-ties in the original box and put it somewhere safe (like your garage or attic) in case something goes wrong and you have to return it.

You probably will not need the manuals and CDs that came with the computer—at least not right away. Put them somewhere safe, though, because if something goes wrong with your computer, you may need those disks and manuals to fix it.

Summary

In this chapter you learned a whole lot about computer hardware and how to choose and set up a new computer with confidence. Even if this information came too late for you (that is, if you already bought your computer without it), at least you can now say that you're well informed, and you'll be ready to buy your *next* computer or help family and friends.

Congratulations on getting this far—learning about all that hardware wasn't easy, especially if you're new to computing. And here's the ironic part—after you have made all the decisions about selecting a computer, and you get it home and get it set up, you really don't need to know much about the hardware. Software is the name of the game from this point on, and it's software we'll be looking at in Chapter 2, "A Crash Course in Windows."

2

A Crash Course in Windows

In this chapter:

- ◆ Starting up and shutting down
- ◆ The Windows desktop
- ◆ Running programs
- ◆ Managing files

Most computers come with Windows XP preinstalled. It's a friendly, easy-to-use system, but if you have never used a computer before, you might find there's a lot to absorb all at once.

This chapter provides a tour of Windows XP and shows you how to do some of the most common activities, such as running programs and copying files. (If you're beyond these basic skills, feel free to skip this chapter!) These skills will serve you well in later chapters, when you get deeper into some of the Windows settings and utilities.

Starting Up and Logging In

The first time you start your new Dell PC, prompts appear that walk you through a setup process. Just follow along with them. After that initial setup, Windows starts automatically each time you turn on your PC.

If you're working with a home computer set up for a single user, Windows logs you in and displays the Windows desktop without you having to do anything.

If you entered multiple user names when you went through the initial setup, or if you have since created other user accounts or set up account passwords, Windows displays a Welcome screen, with names and graphics for each user, as shown in Figure 2.1. You click your own name. If a password is required, a prompt appears for you to enter it. Chapter 3, "Customizing Your Windows Settings," explains how to set up user accounts and passwords.

Click: To move the mouse so its pointer touches an item onscreen, and then press and release the left mouse button once.

If your computer is part of a company network, your network administrator might have set it up for network login, as shown in Figure 2.2. You must enter your user name and password in the boxes provided. (If you don't have a password, you just leave that box blank.)

On some corporate networks, a box might appear prompting you to press Ctrl+Alt+Delete to begin. Hold down Ctrl and Alt and tap the Delete key, and you'll see the network login screen.

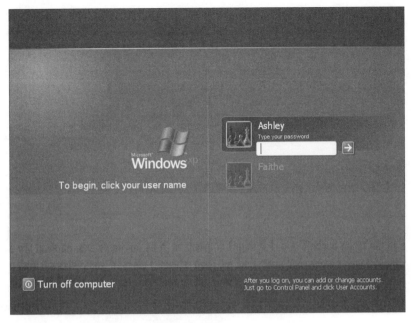

FIGURE 2.1 The Welcome screen in Windows XP.

FIGURE 2.2 The Log On to Windows box appears if the PC has been set up for network login.

You'll know that you have successfully logged in (or that login has occurred automatically) when you see the Windows desktop, as shown in Figure 2.3. Yours might have a different background picture and/or have more icons.

Desktop: The onscreen background, on which various items can be placed. Can also refer to the Windows XP operating environment in general. The picture may be different than the one shown in Figure 2.3.

Icon: A small picture, usually with words underneath it, representing a file, folder, or application.

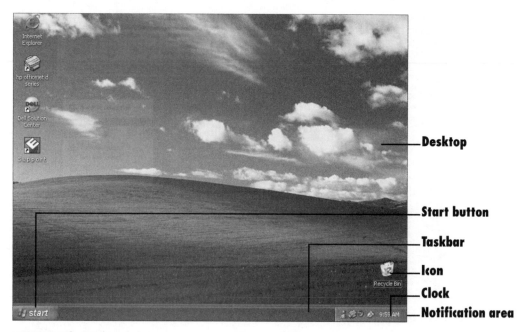

Desktop

Start button

Taskbar

Icon

Clock

Notification area

FIGURE 2.3 The Windows desktop.

Besides the cheerful picture, here's what Figure 2.3 shows:

✦ **Recycle Bin icon.** Here's where files go when you delete them. You can retrieve files from here; I'll explain how later in the chapter.

✦ **Start button.** Click this button to open the menu system from which you can run applications and utilities (also covered later in the chapter).

✦ **Taskbar.** When there are open windows or running programs, their names appear here so you can switch between them easily. In Figure 2.3 there aren't any programs running or windows open, so the taskbar is empty.

✦ **Notification area.** Icons for programs that are running in the background appear here. You might have an icon here for your antivirus program, for example.

✦ **Clock.** This displays the current time. If you point at it with the mouse, a box pops up telling the current date too.

Using a Mouse

If you already know how to use a mouse, you can skip this part. It's just for the brand-new novice users!

The mouse pointer is the white arrow you see on the screen. Move your mouse, and the mouse pointer moves along with it. The mouse pointer is usually a white arrow, but sometimes it changes to other shapes. See Table 2.1 for details.

TABLE 2.1 Mouse Pointers

▷	The normal arrow pointer, used to click (to select) and double-click (to activate).
▷⧗	The hourglass next to the pointer indicates that the system is busy but you can still use the pointer.
⧗	A plain hourglass (no arrow) means that the system is busy and the mouse cannot be used until it is finished.
I	An I-beam indicates that the mouse is over a box in which text can be typed. Click in that box to move an insertion point (a flashing vertical line) there, and then type.
↖↘	A double-headed arrow appears when the mouse pointer is positioned over the border of a resizable window or object. Drag to resize the window or object.
✛	A four-headed arrow appears when the mouse pointer is positioned over the title bar of a movable window or over a movable object, such as an icon. Drag to move the window or object.
👆	A pointing finger appears when the mouse pointer is positioned over a hyperlink, such as on a Web page. Chapter 5, "Getting Started with the Internet," explains hyperlinks.

There are six basic actions you can take with a mouse:

+ **Point.** To move the mouse so that the pointer arrow's tip touches a certain object onscreen.

+ **Click.** To press and release the left mouse button once.

+ **Double-click.** To press and release the left mouse button twice quickly in succession.

+ **Right-click.** To press and release the right mouse button once.

- ✦ **Drag.** To press and hold the left mouse button down, and then move the mouse.
- ✦ **Right-drag.** To press and hold the right mouse button down, and then move the mouse.

TIP

As frivolous as it might sound, one of the best ways for beginners to become accustomed to using a mouse is to play the Solitaire game included with Windows. Solitaire involves a lot of clicking and dragging, and because it's a game that most people already know, it is a confidence builder. In addition, the Minesweeper game that comes with Windows is good for practicing right-clicking.

Restarting the PC

Sometimes when Windows starts acting strangely, such as taking a long time to do simple things or displaying error messages, you can correct the problem by restarting. To restart, do the following:

① Make sure there are no floppy disks in your floppy drive. (They can interfere with the restarting process.)
② Click the Start button. The Start menu opens.
③ Click Shut Down. The shutdown choices in Figure 2.4 or 2.5 appear, depending on how your PC is configured.
④ If what you see looks like Figure 2.4, click Restart. Or, if what you see looks like Figure 2.5, click the down arrow to open the menu (if necessary), and then click Restart. Then, click OK.

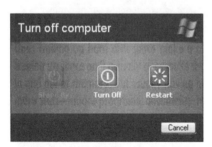

FIGURE 2.4 The default shutdown options in Windows XP.

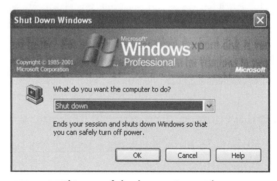

FIGURE 2.5 This type of shutdown options might appear instead.

Shutting Down the PC

When you are finished using your PC, you can leave it on. I know some of you might be hesitant about this, but it's very common to leave a PC on all the time. Really! The PC has power-saving features built in that minimize the amount of electricity it uses.

However, if you are going away for awhile or you need to move the PC or install new hardware, you might want to turn it off completely. Turning off the computer is almost the same as restarting it.

1 Remove any floppy disks from the computer.

> **TIP**
>
> You might also want to remove any CDs, in case you want them while the PC is off, because the Eject button on the CD drive works only while the PC is on.

2 Click the Start button. The Start menu opens.
3 Click Shut Down. The shutdown choices in Figure 2.4 or 2.5 appear, depending on how your PC is configured.
4 If your screen looks like Figure 2.4, click Turn Off. Or, if your screen looks like Figure 2.5, click the down arrow to open the menu, and then click Turn Off. Then click OK.

Working with the Start Menu

Clicking the Start button opens the Start menu, which by default is a two-column affair, as shown in Figure 2.6.

> **TIP**
>
> You can also open the Start menu by pressing the Windows key on your keyboard, if your keyboard has such a key. It looks like this: .

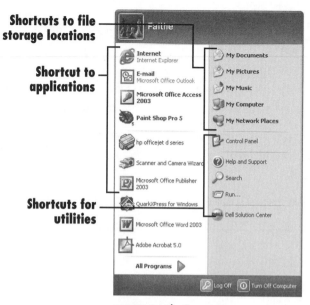

Shortcuts to file storage locations

Shortcut to applications

Shortcuts for utilities

FIGURE 2.6 The Start menu.

On the left side of the Start menu are shortcuts to frequently used applications; you can click any of those to start the application. (You can control what applications appear here, but I'll save that for Chapter 4, "Adding, Removing, and Managing Programs.") There is also an item called All Programs that I'll explain in the "Starting an Application" section later in this chapter.

> **Shortcut:** An icon that serves as a pointer to a file or folder. A single file can have many shortcuts to it in different locations, making access to it more convenient.

On the right side are shortcuts to a variety of file management windows and utilities, many of which you will learn about in upcoming sections and chapters.

Working with Applications

Enough of this background stuff—you probably bought a computer in order to run applications, right? So let's look at how you can start, use, and exit an application. (If you're looking for information on installing applications, see Chapter 4.)

Starting an Application

If a shortcut to the application you want to run appears on the Start menu—great. Just click it to start the application. If it doesn't, you will need to open up the full listing of installed applications and make your selection from there. These are stored in a set of nested menus accessible from All Programs, in the bottom-left corner of the Start menu.

❶ Click the Start button. The Start menu opens.

❷ Point to All Programs. A menu appears. This menu contains a mixture of shortcuts and folders. Each of the folders presents a submenu that opens when you point at it.

❸ If the application you want appears, click its shortcut to start it. Otherwise, navigate through the system of submenus by pointing at menu names until you find the shortcut, and then click it. Figure 2.7 shows several menu levels open.

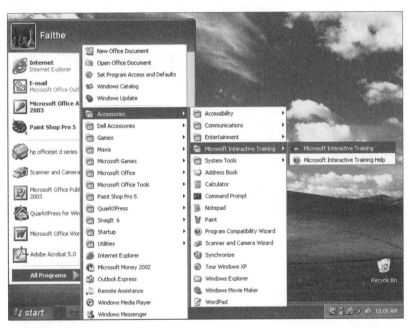

FIGURE 2.7 Shortcuts for running applications can be nested many levels deep on the All Programs menu.

In the remainder of this book, whenever I want you to run a certain application from this menu system, I'll write it with the names of the menus separated by arrows. For example, the path to the Sound Recorder application, illustrated in Figure 2.7, would be written like this: Start > All Programs > Accessories > Entertainment > Sound Recorder.

Depending on the way your PC is set up, you might have shortcut icons on the desktop for various applications. If so, you can double-click one to start that application. It's easier than going through the menu system, hence the name "shortcut." In Chapter 3, "Customizing Your Windows Settings," I'll show you how to create your own shortcuts on the desktop.

Working with an Application Window

When an application runs, it appears in a window. (Almost everything appears in a window, actually; that's why they call it Microsoft Windows.) If you're a novice in Windows, pay close attention to the objects and skills in this section because you will use them over and over with each window you use.

> **Window:** An onscreen box containing an application, a set of options from which to choose, or a listing of files and folders.

The application window has the following parts to it, illustrated in Figure 2.8. If you want to follow along on your own screen, choose Start > All Programs > Accessories > WordPad.

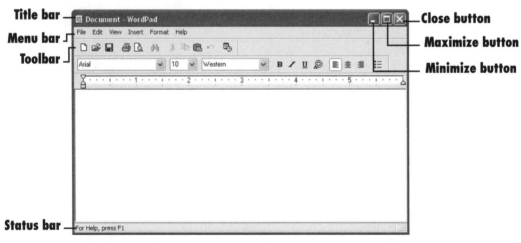

FIGURE 2.8 Parts of a typical application window.

◆ **Title bar.** This is the bar at the top of the window (usually blue) that contains the application's name. For example, in Figure 2.8 the name is WordPad. You can drag the title bar to move the window around on the screen (provided it is not maximized).

◆ **Minimize button.** This button shrinks the application window so it is hidden except for an indicator on the taskbar that shows it is running. This is useful for temporarily getting a window out of your way without closing it.

◆ **Maximize button.** This button enlarges the application window so it fills the entire screen. For some applications, this capability is unavailable so the button appears slightly dimmed. In a window that is already maximized, this button is replaced by a Restore button that puts the window back to its earlier size.

◆ **Close button.** The big red X closes the window entirely and closes the application. If you had any data files open in that application, you are prompted to save them when you click the Close button. (More on this shortly.)

◆ **Menu bar.** Each of the words along the top of the window represents a menu. See the "Selecting from a Menu" section later in the chapter.

◆ **Toolbar.** Many (but not all) applications have a toolbar, which is a series of graphical buttons that represent shortcuts to common menu commands. For example, in Figure 2.8 the Cut button (the one that looks like a pair of scissors) is a shortcut for the Cut command on the Edit menu. Figure 2.8 actually has two toolbars, one below the other. The lower of the two has some drop-down lists as well as regular buttons; to open a drop-down list, click the down arrow to its right.

◆ **Status bar.** Along the bottom of the window is an area where messages from the application to the user appear.

TIP

To move a window, drag its title bar. To resize a window, position the mouse over the bottom-right corner of the window and drag. If the window is maximized, it cannot be moved or resized.

Selecting from a Menu

Click one of the words on the menu bar to open the corresponding menu, and then click a command on the menu to execute it. For example, to exit a program, click File to open the File menu, and then click the Exit command to exit (see Figure 2.9).

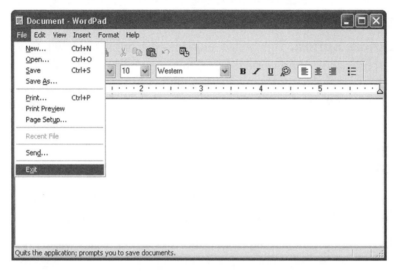

FIGURE 2.9 Click a menu name to open it, and then click a command on the menu.

Sounds simple, huh? And it is, but there are a few tricks to it.

First, you might have noticed that each menu name (and each command) has an underlined letter in it. You can open a menu by holding down the Alt key and typing that letter. Once the menu is open, you can select a command by typing its underlined letter. For example, to exit this program you could press Alt+F (that is, hold down Alt, tap F, and then release Alt), and then type X (because X is the underlined letter in the Exit command).

Also notice in Figure 2.9 that certain commands have key combinations listed next to them, such as Ctrl+P for Print. You can press that key combination instead of opening the menu and selecting the command. (Of course, for this to be of any value, you have to remember the key combination for the command you want. Once you've opened the menu and seen the shortcut keys listed, it's easier to click the desired command than to close the menu and press that key combination.)

In Figure 2.9, the Recent File command is dimmed (also called "grayed out" because it appears gray rather than black). That means the command is not currently available.

Some commands require you to do something else before they are usable. For example, you can't paste until after you have used the cut or copy commands.

The View menu shown in Figure 2.10 illustrates two other menu command variations. The commands in the top portion of the menu are on/off toggles; the ones with check marks next to them are on, and the one without a check mark is off. Each time you select such a command, it switches states.

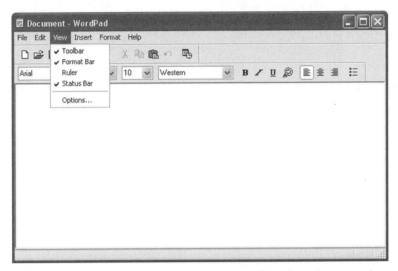

FIGURE 2.10 Another menu example, this one with on/off toggles and a command that opens a dialog box.

The bottom command on the View menu has an ellipsis (…) after it. This indicates that a dialog box will appear when the command is selected.

Dialog box: A window that offers settings to choose from, plus an OK button to accept the settings and a Cancel button to reject the changes.

Making Choices in a Dialog Box

Sometimes a single menu command has many different ways in which it can execute. Take printing, for example. You could print one page, a range, or all pages of a document. You could print one copy or multiple copies. You could print on your default printer or some other printer. In such cases it would not be practical to have a separate menu command for each possibility, so instead there is one general menu command (such as Print) and a dialog box in which you can specify the desired options.

For example, in WordPad you can choose File > Print (that is, open the File menu and click Print) to display the Print dialog box shown in Figure 2.11.

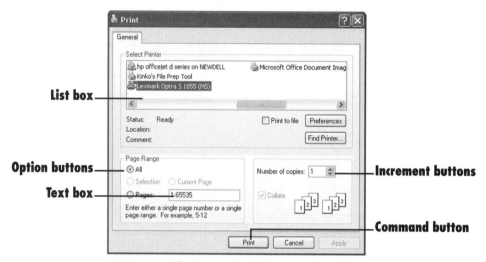

FIGURE 2.11 Dialog boxes such as this one enable you to specify how a command should execute.

Most of the controls in a dialog box are easy to figure out. Here are some of the types shown in Figure 2.11:

♦ **Text box.** Click in it and type.

♦ **Increment buttons.** These little up and down arrows increment the value in a numeric text box. You can use them instead of typing directly into the text box if you wish.

♦ **List box.** This type of control shows the available options (such as the available printers in Figure 2.11); click the one you want.

♦ **Option buttons.** These round buttons are part of a set, like on your car radio. When you click one of them, the previously marked selection is cleared. Notice in Figure 2.11 that the middle option button is grayed out (unavailable).

♦ **Command buttons.** These rounded-rectangle buttons either open a different dialog box (such as the Preferences button in Figure 2.11) or close the current dialog box, either by executing its command (such as the Print button) or canceling it (the Cancel button).

There are a few other dialog box control types besides those shown in Figure 2.11. Figures 2.12 and 2.13 show a couple of other dialog boxes from WordPad that have examples of these types:

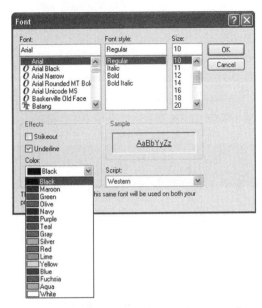

FIGURE 2.12 This dialog box shows check boxes and drop-down lists, plus a scroll bar on a list box. To see this box on your own screen, choose Format > Font.

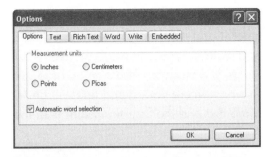

FIGURE 2.13 This dialog box shows tabs. To see this box on your own screen, choose View > Options.

◆ **Check box.** These square boxes are stand-alone yes/no toggles. Unlike option buttons, they are not dependent on any other button's setting.

◆ **Drop-down list.** When you see a text box with a down-pointing arrow at its right, you can click that arrow to open a menu of choices.

◆ **Scroll bar.** When there are too many items in a list box to show onscreen at once, a scroll bar appears to the right of the list. You can use the up and down arrow buttons on it to scroll up and down the list, or drag the scroll box (the rectangular slider on the scroll bar) to move up and down quickly on the list.

◆ **Tabs.** Some dialog boxes have so many choices that they won't all fit in the box. In such cases, multiple tabs are used. Click a tab to move to that "page" of the dialog box.

Entering Data

Different programs have different ways of entering data. For example, the Calculator program (Start > All Programs > Accessories > Calculator) requires you to enter numbers or click number buttons in the application window, whereas the WordPad application shown in Figure 2.8 requires you to type text (or numbers or symbols—whatever).

Some applications give you no choice about where your data will be placed; you simply enter it and it appears in the main data area. (Calculator is like that.) In other applications, you can move an insertion point to control where the data goes. Click where you want the insertion point to appear, and a vertical flashing line appears showing where your typed text will be placed. In Figure 2.14, for example, I have typed some text and the insertion point is at the end of it, waiting for more text to be entered.

Insertion point: A vertical flashing cursor that shows where the text you enter will be placed.

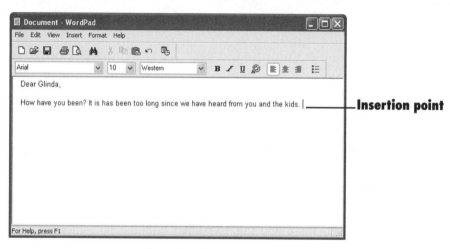

FIGURE 2.14 An insertion point shows where the entered data will appear.

Saving Your Work

As you are working in an application, the data that you enter is stored in RAM. This is temporary storage only; if you exit that application or turn off the computer, whatever was in RAM is cleared and your work is gone.

If you want to preserve your work for later use, you have to save it to a disk. It's usually best to save to your hard disk because that is the most reliable, error-free disk on your PC. Saving to a floppy disk is okay, but floppies tend to develop errors that cause data loss, so you should never save your only copy of a file to a floppy disk. Save the main copy on your hard disk, and then make a backup on a floppy if necessary.

Saving a file writes it to the disk and assigns it a name. (You make up the name yourself. The limit is 255 characters, but you will want to keep the names much shorter than that in most cases, to make them easier to work with.)

CAUTION

On PCs that run the MS-DOS operating system, there is a limitation on file names. They can be no more than eight characters, and they cannot use spaces. If you think you might need to exchange files with someone who uses such a PC (typically a very old computer), make sure your file names conform to those specifications.

Depending on the application, a different file extension will be assigned to the file when you save it. The extension is the three-character code following the period in the file name. The extension is important because it tells Windows which application the file belongs to. For example, Microsoft Word uses the .doc extension for its files, and Microsoft Excel uses .xls. You do not have to type the file extension when you are specifying the name for a new file. The application adds it automatically.

File extension: The file type identifier code following the period in the file's name.

Most disks are organized into multiple folders to keep files separated that have different purposes. (More about folders later, in the "Managing Files" section.) When you save a file, you can choose which disk—and which folder on that disk—in which you want to store the file.

Most applications store data files in a folder called My Documents by default, and for a beginner this is a really good thing because you never have to worry about where your data files are located. They're always in My Documents—end of discussion. Therefore, unless you have a good reason to change it, it's best to stick with the default save location.

Saving in the Default Location

Whew, that was a long warm-up! But you need all that information to make intelligent decisions about saving. Now it's time to give it a try.

To save a file in the default location (in most applications):

1. Choose File > Save or click the Save button on the toolbar (if present). The Save As dialog box appears.
2. Type a name for the file in the Name box (see Figure 2.15).
3. (Optional) If you want to save in a different format than the default, open the Save as Type list and choose a different format.
4. Click Save.

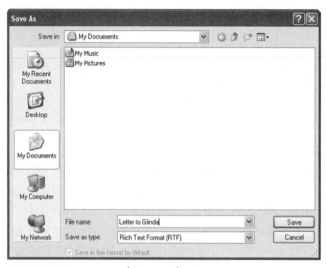

FIGURE 2.15 Save your work in an application.

Saving in Another Location

Here's how to change the save location:

1. From the Save As dialog box, open the Save In drop-down list and choose the drive on which you want to save. A list of folders on that drive appears.
2. Double-click the folder in which you want to save. You might need to do this several times to drill down through several nested layers of folders.
3. Continue saving as normal.

If you don't understand the preceding directions, read the "Managing Files" section later in this chapter, and then come back here and it'll make much more sense.

Resaving an Already Saved File

After you save a file, you can resave it by choosing File > Save again or by clicking on the Save button on the toolbar (if there is one in the application you're using). The file is updated on the disk with the current name, type, and location. No dialog box appears.

If you want to save the file with a different name, type, or location, you must use a different command: File > Save As. This reopens the original Save As dialog box so you can make new selections there.

Opening a Saved File

The whole point of saving a file, of course, is to be able to open it later. Opening copies the file from your disk back into RAM, where the application can use it. The copy on your disk remains untouched until you save again.

To open a file, choose File > Open. In the Open dialog box, click the file to open, and then click OK (or Open, in some applications). The Open dialog box is very much like the Save As dialog box, as you can see in Figure 2.16.

TIP

In some applications, the most recently used files appear at the bottom of the File menu, and you can select them from there to reopen them.

FIGURE 2.16 Open a saved file with File > Open.

Printing Your Work

If you've been following along with everything so far in this chapter, you've already seen how to print because I used the Print dialog box as an example earlier. Choose File > Print, make your choices, and then click OK (or Print, in some applications). Refer back to Figure 2.11 if you want to see the Print dialog box again.

You can also print by clicking on the Print button on the toolbar (if present). However, in most applications this is a different command from File > Print. The toolbar button method prints a single copy of all pages on the default printer, without displaying the Print dialog box.

Exiting an Application

There are several ways to exit an application:

◆ Choose File > Exit.

◆ Click the Close (X) button in the upper-right corner of the application window.

◆ Press Alt+F4. (This works in many, but not all, applications.)

If you have any unsaved work, the application will prompt you to save it.

Managing Files

Files are the basis of almost everything in computing. Whatever you do—whether it's running a program, typing a memo, or optimizing system performance—you are working with files.

Most of the files on your hard disk were placed there when Windows or one of your applications was installed, and they don't require any special handling. The primary reason you will want to work with files is to manage the data files you create using various applications, such as your word processor. You might need to move, copy, or delete those files or change a file's name.

Viewing Files, Folders, and Drives

Folders and drives contain and organize files. Folders are logical dividers that group files together that have a common purpose or type. For example, the files used to run Windows XP are stored in a folder called Windows, and your data files you create in various applications are stored in a folder called My Documents.

In Windows, you are able to see your files, folders, and disks represented as graphic icons in a program called Windows Explorer. From there you can manipulate files and folders by dragging them around. Figure 2.17 shows the Windows Explorer window. To open it, choose Start > All Programs > Accessories > Windows Explorer.

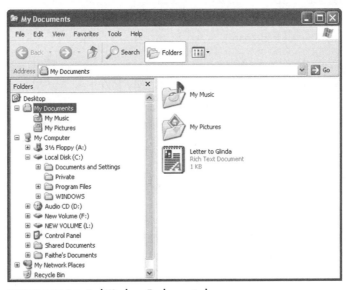

FIGURE 2.17 A typical Windows Explorer window.

In Windows Explorer, there are two panes. On the left is a "tree" showing all the available disk storage on your system; you can click plus signs to expand the branches or minus signs to compress them. On the right is a listing of the files and folders within whatever branch is selected in the left pane. In Figure 2.17, for example, the My Documents folder is selected at the left, and on the right you can see its contents, including the "Letter to Glinda" letter I created earlier in the chapter. You can drag the divider line between the two panes or click the Folders button on the toolbar to turn off the left pane entirely. (Click Folders again to restore the left pane.)

> **TIP**
>
> Notice that the letter does not appear to have any file extension. This is an illusion; it actually has an .rtf extension (which is the default file format for WordPad). By default, Windows hides the file extensions for known file types. If you want to see them, from the Windows Explorer window choose Tools > Folder Options. Click the View tab and clear the Hide Extensions for Known File Types check box.

Now that you have seen how to turn the folder tree pane on and off, I'll let you in on a little secret: There's an easier way to open Windows Explorer. Choose Start > My Computer. This opens up Windows Explorer, but without the folder tree. If you then click the Folders button, you're right there where you would have been if you had used the longer path (Start > All Programs > Accessories > Windows Explorer).

Go back and take another look at the upper-right corner of the Start menu, and notice the various locations listed there: My Documents, My Pictures, My Music, My Computer, and My Network Places. Each of these is a shortcut to Windows Explorer; the only difference is the folder that you start in. It's all starting to fit together, isn't it?

Navigating between Folders

Once you've opened a file management window, you can display the content of any drive or folder. One of the easiest ways to switch to a different folder is simply to click its name in the folder tree (left pane). If you don't see a folder you want, click a plus sign to expand a tree branch.

Think of the folder tree as a branching root system in which you start off with the disk at the top (the parent folder, also called the *root folder*), and then you have child folders beneath it, and then children of children within those, and so on.

Moving up in the system means moving closer to the root folder organizationally. To move up one level, click the Up One Level button in the Windows Explorer toolbar, or simply click the desired folder in the folder tree (see Figure 2.18).

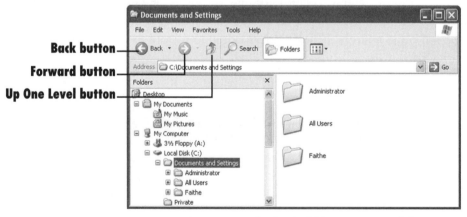

FIGURE 2.18 To move up one level in the folder organization, click Up One Level.

Moving down means moving into a subordinate folder within the current one. To move down one level, double-click a folder in the right pane or click the plus sign next to a folder in the left pane to expand it, and then click one of its subordinate folders.

When you display a different location's contents, whatever was in the right pane is replaced. If you want to return to the previously displayed content, click the Back button (see Figure 2.18). If you want to move ahead again to the display as it was before you clicked Back, click the Forward button. This is just like in a Web browser (see Chapter 5).

TIP

If you know the full path to the desired location, you can type it in the Address bar and press Enter to jump to it.

Selecting Files and Folders

As I mentioned earlier, the primary reason most people open a file management window is to do something to a data file they've created. For example, you might want to delete a letter or copy it to a floppy disk.

Before you can act on a file, you must select it. No matter what the activity, it's always a two-part equation, like a subject-verb sentence: First you select what you want to act on (the subject), and then you choose the activity to perform (the verb).

To select a single file or folder, click it. To deselect it, click somewhere away from it. A selected file appears in white letters with a dark background—the opposite of an unselected one.

You can select multiple files or folders and act on them as a group. For example, if you needed to delete 10 different files in the same folder, you could select them all and issue the Delete command once. Here are some ways to select multiple files:

✦ To select a contiguous group (that is, all together in the listing), click the first file, hold down the Shift key, and click the last file.

✦ To select non-contiguous files, hold down the Ctrl key as you click each file.

✦ To select a contiguous block of files, drag a box around the group with your mouse pointer (holding down the left mouse button as you drag) to "lasso" them.

Moving and Copying Files and Folders

Now that you know how to select files and folders, it's time to learn what you can do to them. Two very common activities are moving and copying. You could copy a file to a floppy disk to share with a friend, for example, or move some old data files to a backup disk for storage.

Here are some methods for moving a file or folder (or a group of them):

◆ **Drag-and-drop.** Select the items to move in the right pane, and then drag them and drop them onto a folder in the folder tree (left pane). If you are moving from one disk to another, you must hold down the Shift key as you drag. (Otherwise, Windows will copy rather than move.)

◆ **Cut and paste.** Select the items to move, and then choose Edit > Cut or press Ctrl+X. Display the destination location, and then choose Edit > Paste or press Ctrl+V.

◆ **Move to Folder command.** Select the items to move in the right pane, and then choose Edit > Move to Folder. In the Move Items dialog box, select the destination folder and click the Move button (see Figure 2.19).

FIGURE 2.19 Use the Move Items dialog box to select a destination.

Copying works nearly the same way:

◆ **Drag-and-drop.** Select the items to move in the right pane, and then hold down the Ctrl key and drag them and drop them onto a folder in the folder tree (left pane). If you are moving from one disk to another, you do not have to hold down Ctrl (although it doesn't hurt anything to do so).

◆ **Copy and paste.** Select the items to move, and then choose Edit > Copy or press Ctrl+C. Display the destination location, and then choose Edit > Paste or press Ctrl+V.

◆ **Copy to Folder command.** Select the items to move in the right pane, and then choose Edit > Copy to Folder. In the Copy Items dialog box, select the destination folder and click the Copy button.

2

Deleting Files and Folders

You will probably want to delete old data files that you no longer have any use for to save space on your hard disk and make it easier to locate the data files you currently need.

To delete one or more files or folders, select them and then perform any of the following actions:

◆ Press the Delete key.

◆ Click the Delete button on the toolbar.

◆ Choose File > Delete.

◆ Drag the files to the Recycle Bin icon on the desktop and drop them there.

A confirmation box appears; click Yes to delete the files.

Renaming Files and Folders

Many beginning computer users give their data files rather generic names, such as Letter1, Letter2, and so on. They don't realize that over time they will probably create hundreds of letters, and it will be difficult to sort them out. You can rename a file easily in Windows to give it a better or more descriptive name.

CAUTION

Don't rename files or folders needed to run a program, or the program might not work anymore. Rename only data files and folders that you have created yourself.

To rename a file or folder, select it and then press the F2 key. The name becomes selected. Type a new name and press Enter.

Do you need to type the file extension when renaming? It depends on whether file extensions are displayed or not. If they are not, then don't type the file extension. If they are displayed, then do. If file extensions are not displayed and you type an extension, the file will end up with two extensions in its name, such as Letter.rtf.rtf. If file extensions are displayed and you don't type an extension, you will get an error about changing the file type.

Creating New Folders

As your My Documents folder begins to fill up with data files, you might find that you want to bring some organization to them. One excellent way to do so is to create new folders within My Documents and then drag-and-drop your data files into the appropriate folder.

To create a folder, display the folder that the new folder should be inside (for example, My Documents), and then choose File > New > Folder. A new folder appears, with the name "New Folder." The name is highlighted and ready to be typed over with a new name. Do so, and then press Enter. If you accidentally press Enter before you type the new name, rename the folder as explained in the preceding section.

Working with the Recycle Bin

Deleting a file does not immediately destroy it in Windows. And believe me, there will be times when you will be very grateful for this fact! Instead the deleted files and folders go to a special folder called the Recycle Bin. There's a shortcut to it on your desktop for easy access. You can restore a deleted file from the Recycle Bin much as you can fish a piece of paper out of a wastebasket.

To open the Recycle Bin, double-click its icon on the desktop. A window opens showing its contents, much like a regular file management window.

Select the file you want to restore. In Figure 2.20, I've selected Assign6.xls. Then, click Restore This Item in the Recycle Bin Tasks area at the left. The file goes back where it came from originally.

> **TIP**
>
> You can drag the file out of the Recycle Bin and onto the desktop (or into any other file management window) to restore it there. This is useful if you don't remember where the file originally came from and you don't want to have to go digging for it.

FIGURE 2.20 Select a file in the Recycle Bin to restore it.

As with other file management windows, you can select multiple files and/or folders at once in the Recycle Bin window, and you can restore them in a single step.

Windows automatically empties the Recycle Bin when disk space gets low, but you can also empty it yourself (for privacy, for example). To do so, right-click the Recycle Bin icon on the desktop and choose Empty Recycle Bin. Or, if the Recycle Bin window is already open, click Empty the Recycle Bin in the Recycle Bin Tasks pane at the left.

3

Customizing Your Windows Settings

In this chapter:

◆ Changing display settings

◆ Exploring the Control Panel options

◆ Sharing your PC with multiple users

Windows XP works pretty well right out of the starting gate, but perhaps there are a few things you would like to change about it. If so, you've come to the right place. In this chapter, I'll show you some easy ways to make Windows your own.

Changing Display Settings

The display is your computer's primary method of communicating with you, so you will spend a tremendous amount of time looking at it. Taking a few minutes to adjust its settings to match your preferences can deliver big dividends in comfort and enjoyment.

Setting the Background Image

Let's start with the background picture on the desktop. Don't like it? Change it! You can use any picture or no picture at all.

To change the background image:

1. Right-click the desktop and choose Properties. The Display Properties dialog box opens.
2. Click the Desktop tab.
3. Click a different picture or choose None to turn the picture off entirely. A preview of your new setting appears in the sample area, as shown in Figure 3.1.

FIGURE 3.1 Select a picture to appear as the desktop background.

TIP

The pictures that appear on this list are stored in the Windows folder or the My Pictures folder. You can select a picture from a different location by clicking the Browse button and locating/selecting the picture you want. See Chapter 7, "Working with Scanners, Cameras, and Printers" for information about getting pictures into your computer.

④ Open the Position drop-down list and choose a position:
+ **Stretch.** Enlarges the image so it fits the desktop exactly.
+ **Center.** If the picture is smaller than the desktop, a single copy of the picture appears in the center. This is good for situations when the Stretch setting distorts the picture unacceptably.
+ **Tile.** If the picture is smaller than the desktop, multiple copies are laid side by side to cover the desktop. This is good for small pictures.
⑤ (Optional) Open the Color drop-down list and choose a background color. If you chose Center in Step 4, this color will appear around the edges of the picture if it is smaller than the desktop. If you chose None in Step 3, this will be the solid color that fills the entire desktop. This isn't necessary if you chose Stretch or Tile in Step 4 because the background color will not be visible.
⑥ Click OK. The new image is applied to the desktop.

TIP

Here's a quick way to set the background image: From a file management window (such as My Computer), right-click a picture file and choose Set as Desktop Background.

Appearance Settings

If you used earlier versions of Windows before Windows XP, you probably noticed that Windows XP has a whole different look to it. The windows have rounded corners and thick blue title bars, for example. That's the Windows XP *theme*. Windows XP also comes with an alternative theme called Windows Classic. It makes the Windows environment look very much like earlier versions, with more squared-off windows and plainer effects. You can also download additional themes online.

Theme: A collection of appearance settings saved under a common name.

To switch between the available themes follow these steps:

① Right-click the desktop and choose Properties. The Display Properties dialog box opens.

② Click the Themes tab (see Figure 3.2).

FIGURE 3.2 Choose a theme for your Windows display.

③ Open the Theme drop-down list and choose the desired theme.

TIP

Choose More Themes Online in Step 3 to look for more themes on the Internet. Choose Browse in Step 3 to locate and use a theme that is stored elsewhere on your computer.

---

④ Click OK. The new theme is applied.
OR
If you want to keep experimenting, click Apply instead, and then skip to Step 2 of the following procedure.

You can adjust the settings involved in the theme individually. This enables you to start with a certain theme and make custom changes. Here's how:

① Right-click the desktop and choose Properties. The Display Properties dialog box opens.

② Click the Appearance tab (see Figure 3.3).

③ Open the Windows and Buttons drop-down list and choose Windows XP Style or Windows Classic Style.

④ Open the Color Scheme drop-down list and choose a color scheme. There are many more choices if you choose Windows Classic in Step 3 than if you choose Windows XP.

FIGURE 3.3 Choose appearance settings for your display.

⑤ Open the Font Size drop-down list and choose a font size for screen elements—Normal, Large, or Extra Large.
⑥ Click OK.

TIP

You can also click the Effects button and choose from a dialog box of effect settings. You can click Advanced to customize the color scheme even further, specifying colors for each onscreen element. Experiment with these settings on your own if desired.

Resolution and Color Depth

The display in Windows is composed of thousands of tiny, colored dots called *pixels*. The *resolution* is the number of individual pixels that make up a particular display mode. It is expressed in width times height, such as 800×600 (the default resolution).

Pixel: A colored dot on the display.

If you choose a higher resolution, everything onscreen (except the desktop itself) will appear smaller. Why? Because at a higher resolution, the dots are smaller and closer together, and most objects have a specific size measured in pixels. If a particular icon is 20 pixels wide, it's going to look smaller in 1024×768 resolution than in 800×600 resolution because in the former, the physical space of the screen is divided into 1024 unique pixels, while in the latter that same physical space is divided into only 800 pixels.

Display resolution is largely a matter of personal preference. Some people like things to be large so they can see them better, especially on a small monitor. Other people like to be able to cram a lot onscreen at once.

Color quality (a.k.a. *color depth*) can also be adjusted for the display. You can choose between Medium (16-bit) and Highest (32-bit). Those numbers refer to the number of binary digits required to uniquely describe each possible color that a particular pixel can be. With 16-bit color, there are 2^{16} (65,536) colors to choose from. With 32-bit color, there are 2^{32} (4,294,967,296). A lower color depth can slightly increase the video display performance because less data must be transferred between the PC and its video display. Most people cannot tell a difference between the two modes except when working with photographs (and even then, the difference is not very apparent).

To change the resolution and color quality, follow these steps:

❶ Right-click the desktop and choose Properties. The Display Properties dialog box opens.

❷ Click the Settings tab (see Figure 3.4).

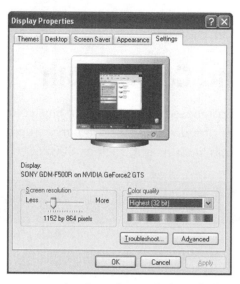

FIGURE 3.4 Adjust the resolution and color quality here.

③ Drag the Screen Resolution slider to the left or right to adjust its setting.

④ Open the Color Quality drop-down list and make your selection there.

⑤ Click OK.

If this is the first time you have tried a particular setting, a confirmation box might appear. Click OK or Yes to move past it.

Refresh Rate

Have you ever noticed that some computer monitors are much easier on the eyes than others? One reason for this is the *refresh rate*.

Refresh rate: The rate at which the pixels on the display are refreshed.

A CRT monitor (see Chapter 1) works by firing an electron gun at phosphorescent coating on the inside of the monitor to make it glow. As soon as the phosphor is hit, it immediately begins decaying back to black, so the monitor has to hit each phosphor many times per second. The number of times per second each phosphor is refreshed is the refresh rate. If the refresh rate is too low, you will notice a flicker on the display that will make your eyes tired. If the refresh rate is set higher than the monitor can keep up with, it can damage the monitor.

The maximum refresh rate depends on the monitor's capabilities and on the display resolution you have chosen (refer to the preceding section). If Windows correctly detects your monitor, then it also correctly detects its maximum refresh rate; if it is unable to detect your monitor, Windows plays it safe and uses a low refresh rate.

To change the refresh rate:

① Right-click the desktop and choose Properties. The Display Properties dialog box opens.

② Click the Settings tab, and then click the Advanced button. The properties for your video card and monitor appear.

③ Click the Monitor tab. If the correct monitor is not shown there, click the Properties button and specify the correct monitor model.

④ After you confirm the monitor is correct, open the Screen Refresh Rate drop-down list and choose the desired rate (see Figure 3.5). If Optimal is one of the choices, use that; otherwise, choose a specific refresh rate that you know your monitor can support. (Check its documentation.) The higher the better, as long as you don't go past the monitor's capability.

⑤ Click OK, and then click OK again to save your changes. If a confirmation box appears, click OK or Yes to dismiss it.

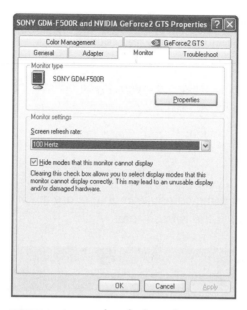

FIGURE 3.5 Increase the refresh rate for a more flicker-free display.

Setting the Date and Time

Have you ever wondered how your computer always seems to know the date and time? It's because of a clock built into the motherboard (called a *real-time clock*). There's a small battery on the motherboard that keeps this clock powered when you turn off the computer.

If you move to a different time zone, or if your computer's clock starts losing time, you can adjust the date and time through Windows. Just double-click the clock on the taskbar to display the Date and Time Properties dialog box, and from there choose the correct date and time (see Figure 3.6). Click OK when you're finished.

If you have changed time zones, choose your new zone on the Time Zone tab.

TIP

You can tell Windows to keep the clock updated for you automatically by using a time server on the Internet. To do this, display the Internet Time tab and make sure the Automatically Synchronize with an Internet Time Server check box is selected.

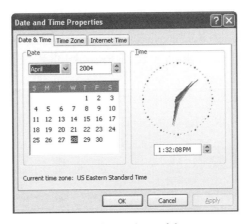

FIGURE 3.6 Set the date and time if they are inaccurate.

Exploring the Control Panel

Almost all the devices on your system have properties you can control, and the Control Panel is a one-stop shop for them. To open the Control Panel, choose Start > Control Panel.

By default the Control Panel appears in Category view, as shown in Figure 3.7. It simplifies the controls by breaking them down into logical categories. Some people

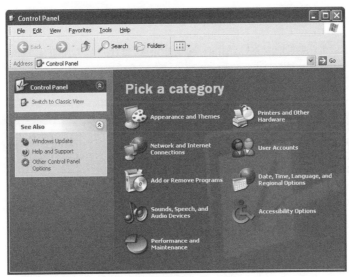

FIGURE 3.7 Control panel, Category view.

have a hard time finding what they need this way, though, so you might prefer Classic view (see Figure 3.8), in which every available device has its own separate icon. Click the Switch to Classic View link in the left pane to make the change.

FIGURE 3.8 Control panel, Classic view.

To select a category in Category view, click it. A list of items in that category appears; click the one you want.

To select an icon in Classic view, double-click it.

NOTE

The icons in your Control Panel might be different from the ones shown in Figure 3.8. That is normal. The icons shown depend on what hardware and system utilities are installed.

Plug-and-Play: A technology that enables Windows to automatically detect new hardware and install drivers for it with little or no user intervention.

Each of the items in the Control Panel opens a Properties box for a particular piece of hardware or system capability. Table 3.1 summarizes the items shown in Figure 3.8.

TABLE 3.1 Control Panel Utilities

Item	Notes
Accessibility Options	Use these to turn on and off features that make Windows easier to use for people with vision, hearing, or mobility limitations.
Add Hardware	This runs a setup wizard that helps you set up new hardware. It is not usually necessary because most new hardware is *Plug-and-Play*.
Add or Remove Programs	This utility helps you install and uninstall software. You will use it extensively in Chapter 4, "Adding, Removing, and Managing Programs."
Administrative Tools	Ignore these; they are for advanced users. They enable you to view various system settings and status reports.
Date and Time	This is the same as double-clicking the clock to access the date and time settings, as you learned how to do earlier.
Display	This is the same as right-clicking the desktop and choosing Properties, as you learned how to do earlier.
Folder Options	Here you can control the settings for file management windows, as you learned in Chapter 2. You can also access these same options by choosing Tools > Folder Options from any file management window.
Fonts	This folder shows all the fonts installed on your system and enables you to install or delete fonts. This is mostly for advanced users.
Game Controllers	If you have any game controllers, you can adjust them here.
Internet Options	Here you can control the settings for Internet Explorer, the default Web browser software that comes with Windows. You can also access these same options by choosing Tools > Internet Options from Internet Explorer. You will look at some of these options in Chapter 6, "Ensuring Your Security and Privacy Online."
Keyboard	You can set the repeat rate and repeat delay, which control what happens when you hold down a certain key. (Ever held down the period on an electric typewriter and watched a row of periods zoom onto the page? It's a similar concept.)
Mouse	You can change the appearance of the mouse pointers, adjust the mouse pointer sensitivity (that is, how far the pointer moves onscreen in relation to how far you move the mouse itself), and adjust the double-click rate (that is, how fast the two clicks have to be in order to be considered a double-click). You can also switch the button functionality, which is great for left-handed people who want to use their strongest finger for the main button.

3

TABLE 3.1 Continued

Item	Notes
Network Connections	You can view and manage your network connectivity here. You'll learn about networking in Chapter 10, "Setting Up a Home Network."
Phone and Modem Options	You can configure your telephone settings here (such as whether you have touch or pulse service, and what your area code is), and check any modems you have installed.
Power Options	These settings enable you to save electricity when your PC is idle by turning off the monitor and hard disks after a specified period of inactivity.
Printers and Faxes	This opens a window showing all the installed printers and fax drivers on your system. You can change which one is the default, and you can view and manage their queues. Chapter 7, "Working with Scanners, Cameras, and Printers," will cover these options.
Regional and Language Options	These settings enable you to set up Windows for use in other countries. No, they don't change the language in which prompts appear in Windows—you would need a whole different version of Windows for that. However, they do set the currency symbol and the date and time formats to match those customarily used in the chosen country.
Scanners and Cameras	If you have any scanners or digital cameras installed, you can manage their settings here. You'll look more at this in Chapter 7.
Scheduled Tasks	You can schedule programs to run at certain dates and times with this utility. It's useful for creating maintenance schedules that involve running certain maintenance utilities, such as Backup and Disk Defragmenter. Chapter 9, "Cleaning and Maintaining Your PC," explains some of the utilities you might want to schedule.
Sounds and Audio Devices	If you have speakers, digital instruments, sound cards, voice synthesizers, and other audio devices installed, you can manage their settings here. You can also adjust the volume control here, and specify whether a volume control icon will appear in the notification area (recommended).
Speech	If you have software installed for voice recognition or text-to-speech conversion, you can manage the settings here.
System	This opens the System Properties box, in which you can make some rather advanced-level changes to the way Windows operates. Beginners, please don't experiment here!

TABLE 3.1 Continued

Item	Notes
Taskbar and Start Menu	This set of properties enables you to change how the taskbar and the Start menu look and operate.
User Accounts	Here you can set up user profiles so that multiple people can use the same PC with some semblance of privacy. See the following section to learn more.

Sharing Your PC with Multiple Users

In most homes, there are several people using the same computer. Besides the obvious fights over who gets to use the PC first, there can also be privacy issues, especially when there are teenagers involved!

Windows enables you to set up multiple user accounts, each of which has its own separate My Documents folder and Favorites list (in Internet Explorer—see Chapter 5, "Getting Started with the Internet"). That way, private documents can be kept private.

Logging In with Multiple Users

When multiple users are set up in Windows, each time the PC starts up the Welcome screen appears (refer to Figure 2.1 from Chapter 2). You click on your user name and enter a password if prompted, and then Windows finishes starting up by loading your personal settings. Or, if the Welcome screen feature is turned off, instead you see a prompt like the one from Figure 2.2 from Chapter 2, in which you must type your user name and password.

> **TIP**
>
> To get rid of the login screen so that Windows starts up automatically, you must do *all* of the following: 1) Delete all user profiles except one. 2) Remove the password from the remaining profile. 3) Disable the Guest account.

Setting Up User Accounts

The first time you started up your brand-new computer, you were probably prompted to enter your name and the names of anyone else who would be using the PC. These were used to create user accounts. Therefore, you might already have several user accounts in place.

First, open the User Accounts window (see Figure 3.9) from the Control Panel. The existing users appear in the Or Pick an Account to Change section. In Figure 3.9, for example, there are two users: Ashley and Faithe.

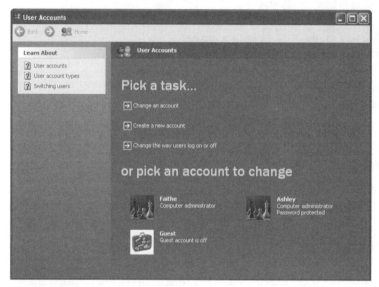

FIGURE 3.9 Manage user accounts here.

To add an account, follow these steps:

1 Click Create a New Account.

2 Type the name of the person and click Next.

3 Choose the type of account you want: Computer Administrator or Limited. Users with Computer Administrator privileges have free access to change anything about the computer's configuration; those with Limited privileges can only run applications and change their own password.

4 Click Create Account.

You can delete unwanted accounts, but be careful. When you delete an account, all the documents created by that user can be deleted, too. Make sure you choose Keep Files in Step 3 of the following process to retain any documents.

To delete an account:

① Click the account you want to delete.
② Click Delete the Account.
③ If you plan to move this user's settings to another computer, choose Keep Files. This will create a folder on the desktop with that user's name, containing the user's documents and desktop shortcuts. If you won't need that user's documents and settings, click Delete Files.

Working with Account Passwords

If privacy is a concern, you will want to assign passwords to each account so nobody can use anyone else's login. Here's how to assign a password to an account:

① Click the account for which you want to set a password.
② Click Create a Password.
③ Type the password in the Type a New Password text box, and then do so again in the Type the New Password Again to Confirm text box.
④ (Optional) If you want to provide a password hint, enter it in the Type a Word or Phrase to Use as a Password Hint text box.
⑤ Click Create Password.
⑥ Click Back to return to the User Accounts window.

Removing a password disables the password protection for the account so it is once again freely accessible to anyone. To remove a password:

① Click the account for which you want to remove the password.
② Click Remove the Password.
③ Some information appears regarding losing personal certificates and stored passwords. Read it, and then click Remove Password.

Security experts recommend changing a password occasionally for added security. You might want to change your password every month or so if you are worried about others guessing it. To change a password:

① Click the account for which you want to change the password.
② Click Change the Password.
③ Enter a new password in the Type a New Password text box, and then type it again in the Type the New Password Again to Confirm text box.
④ (Optional) Enter a password hint in the Type a Word or Phrase to Use as a Password Hint text box.
⑤ Click Change Password.

Switching Users

If Fast User Switching is enabled, you can switch to a different user without the first user having to shut everything down. This can be handy if one person is working on the computer and another one comes up and wants to use it for a minute.

First, check to see whether Fast User Switching is enabled. From the User Accounts window, follow these steps:

1. Click Change the Way Users Log On or Off.
2. Make sure that Use the Welcome Screen is marked.
3. Make sure that Use Fast User Switching is marked.
4. Click Apply Options.

Now, click Start>Log Off. The Log Off Windows box appears (see Figure 3.10). In it, click Switch User. This takes you back to the Welcome screen so another user can log in. The previous user is still logged in, and you can repeat the Switch User process again to get back to that user at any time; the applications and windows that were open before will still be open.

FIGURE 3.10 Choose to log off or switch users.

Logging On and Off

The procedure described in the preceding section is not really logging off. When a real log-off occurs, everything that the user was doing gets shut down, including applications and file windows. (Log-off occurs automatically when you shut down or restart, as described in Chapter 2.)

In a school or business situation, you will probably want to log off for your own protection before you leave the computer workstation. To log off, click Start>Log Off, and then click the Log Off button.

If the Welcome screen and Fast User Switching are not both enabled, when you log off you will see a different prompt. Instead of the one shown in Figure 3.10, you will see something like Figure 3.11. Click Log Off to complete the log-off.

FIGURE 3.11 Log off when Fast User Switching is not enabled.

3

4

Adding, Removing, and Managing Programs

In this chapter:

◆ Installing new programs

◆ Removing programs

◆ Setting up program shortcuts

Most computers come with at least a dozen programs pre-installed—everything from music editors to word processors and games. If your needs happen to match up with those pre-installed programs, great! But if not, you might find you need to buy and install some different programs. In addition, you might want to remove any of the pre-installed programs that you don't want in order to save hard disk space. In this chapter, you will learn how to add and remove programs, as well as how to create shortcuts to your programs.

Installing New Software

Most programs that you buy come on a compact disc (CD) that contains a Setup utility. You run this Setup utility to install the program on your computer.

This Setup utility (see Figure 4.1) does several important things:

◆ It copies the files needed for running the program to your hard disk.

◆ It creates a *shortcut* to the program on the Start menu. It might also place another shortcut for the program directly on the desktop.

Shortcut: A pointer to the original file. Double-clicking on the shortcut retrieves the file to which it points.

◆ It adds information about the program to the Windows *Registry*.

Registry: A configuration file that tells Windows about your hardware, software, and system settings. Each time Windows starts, it reads and applies these settings.

It's Automatic

When you insert the CD for a new program in your computer, a prompt will probably appear automatically for installing the software. If so, just follow along with the prompts. This kind of automatic prompting is made possible by a Windows feature called *Autoplay*. Each time you insert a CD, Windows looks on that CD for a file called Autorun.inf. If Windows finds such a file, it executes the instructions it finds there. Those instructions display a menu that enables you to install and/or run the program, as shown in Figure 4.2.

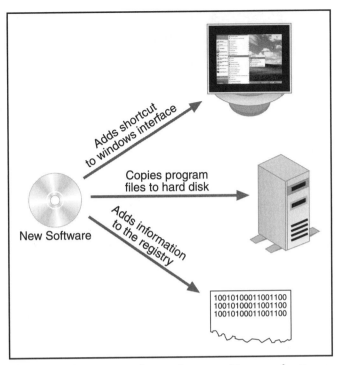

FIGURE 4.1 Software setup utilities perform several important functions automatically.

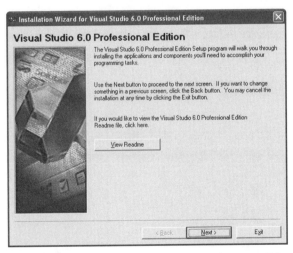

FIGURE 4.2 Many programs distributed on CD offer to install themselves automatically when you insert the CD in your computer.

Autoplay: A Windows feature that enables a program on a CD-ROM to run automatically when you insert the CD.

If nothing happens when you insert the CD, maybe it doesn't have an Autorun.inf file (some don't), or maybe your computer's CD drive is not set up for Autoplay. That's okay, though; the next sections will provide you with alternative methods.

> **NOTE**
>
> Autoplay is turned on by default in Windows XP. If you don't want Autoplay to operate in a specific instance, hold down the Shift key as you insert the CD. To change the Autoplay setting for a drive, display My Computer, right-click the drive, and make your selection on the Autoplay tab in the drive's Properties box.

Browsing for Setup on Your Own

If Autoplay doesn't provide you with an automatic menu, don't sweat it. It's easy to manually find and start the Setup utility yourself. More than 90 percent of the time, it is named Setup.exe and it is located in the top-level folder on the CD, so give these steps a try:

1. Choose Start > My Computer. The My Computer window opens.
2. Double-click the icon for the CD drive. Depending on how the CD is set up, either the Autoplay menu opens (in which case you're back to where you were with the automatic method in the preceding section) or a list of the files on the CD appears, as in Figure 4.3.

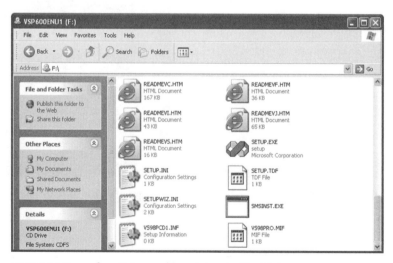

FIGURE 4.3 Browse for a Setup.exe file and then double-click it.

③ Browse through the list of files on the CD and double-click Setup.exe.

④ Follow the prompts to complete the setup.

You might occasionally run into a program for which the setup file is not named Setup.exe. In that case, you will have to make an educated guess about which file starts setup, or you can let Windows identify it for you (more on that in the following section).

If you decide to try to identify it yourself, look for an icon that shows a picture of a computer with an open software box next to it, as shown in Figure 4.4. This icon is traditionally used for the file that starts a program's setup.

TIP

The setup file will have an .exe extension on it, as shown in Figure 4.4, but Windows might not be set up to show extensions. To show the extensions, from My Computer open the Tools menu and choose Folder Options, and then clear the Hide Extensions for Known File Types check box on the View tab.

FIGURE 4.4 If there is no Setup.exe, look for a file with this icon.

Letting Windows Find the Setup Program

Occasionally, you might run into a snag with the preceding procedure. Perhaps there's no Setup.exe on the CD, or perhaps the CD has several folders on it and you're not sure which one to search. You can poke around on your own looking for Setup.exe, or you can let Windows locate the correct file for you automatically.

To ask Windows to look for the appropriate setup utility for the new program, follow these steps:

① Choose Start > Control Panel.

② Click Add or Remove Programs (see Figure 4.5).

NOTE

Figure 4.5 shows the Control Panel in Category view, the default. If yours is displayed in Classic view (a white background with icons), double-click Add New Programs in Step 2.

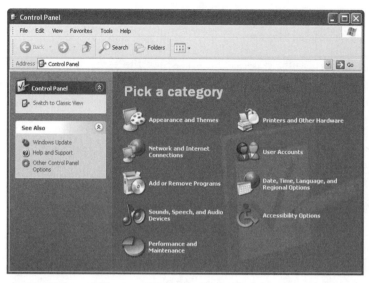

FIGURE 4.5 Choose Add or Remove Programs in the Control Panel.

❸ Click Add New Programs.

❹ Click the CD or Floppy button.

❺ Make sure the CD for the program is in your CD drive, and then click Next. (See Figure 4.6.) Windows attempts to find the appropriate file for the Setup utility.

❻ Click Finish. The Setup utility runs. From this point, just follow the prompts.

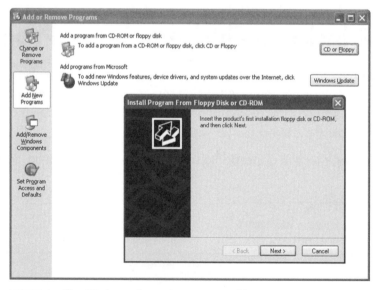

FIGURE 4.6 Allow Windows to locate the appropriate file.

Tips for Installing Older Software

The software you buy in stores today is designed for Windows XP, so you should have no trouble installing and running it. However, if you have old software you bought before Windows XP was released (that is, prior to 2001), it might not work perfectly (or at all) on Windows XP.

If you see a warning like the one in Figure 4.7 during or after setup, check the program manufacturer's Web site to see whether an update to the program is available. There might be something you can download and install that will fix the incompatibility. (See Chapter 5 to learn how to use the Web.)

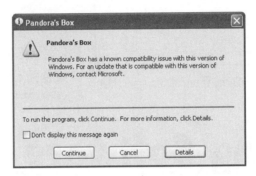

FIGURE 4.7 Some older programs require updates to work with Windows XP.

Another possible solution might be to use the *Program Compatibility Wizard* feature in Windows to troubleshoot version-related problems. It enables you to specify which version of Windows to emulate when your system is running that program.

Program Compatibility Wizard: A feature that helps you set up Windows XP to run software designed for earlier Windows versions.

To run the Wizard, choose Start > All Programs > Program Compatibility Wizard. From this point, simply follow the step-by-step prompts. Figure 4.8 shows one of the steps in the process.

More advanced users might prefer to configure compatibility without the Wizard. To do this, right-click on the shortcut to the program and choose Properties, and then set compatibility options on the Compatibility tab (see Figure 4.9).

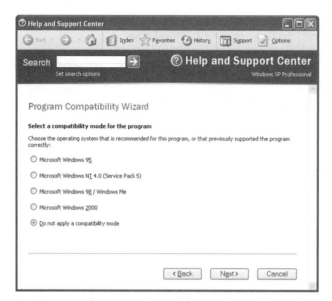

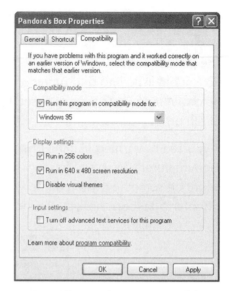

FIGURE 4.8 Use the Program Compatibility Wizard to configure older programs to run under Windows XP.

FIGURE 4.9 You can also set up compatibility options without the Wizard.

Removing Software

It's not strictly necessary, but it's a good housekeeping idea to remove software that you never use to free up space on your hard disk.

NOTE

Does freeing up hard disk space make a computer run faster? Not usually. In cases when the hard disk is very full, freeing up space on it actually *does* make the computer run faster because there is more room for Windows to swap data in and out of memory. But usually having hard disk space available is desirable mainly because it enables you to store more stuff—more programs, documents, music clips, videos, and so on.

Removing certain types of programs provides additional benefits. If a particular program loads automatically each time Windows starts up, removing it can make the computer start up more quickly.

The software removal (uninstallation) process reverses all three of the things done during installation:

✦ It deletes the files that were stored on the hard disk for the program.

- ✦ It removes the program's shortcuts from the Start menu and desktop.
- ✦ It removes any entries in the Registry pertaining to the program.

CAUTION

Some people try to remove software by simply deleting the files manually from the hard disk, but that accomplishes only the first of the three aforementioned processes. The shortcuts for starting the program still exist, but they no longer work. And the entries in the Registry for the program remain. Normally those orphaned entries don't cause problems, but they do make the Registry larger than necessary so Windows takes longer to start up than it otherwise might.

4

Removing Programs That Have Uninstall Utilities

Some programs put a shortcut for self-removal on the Start menu. This makes the process very easy—you simply select that shortcut and follow the prompts. Figure 4.10 shows an example.

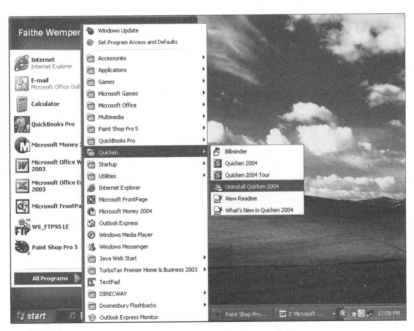

FIGURE 4.10 If a program has its own uninstall utility, that's the best way to remove it.

A few programs require you to have the original CD for the program in your PC in order to uninstall. You'll be prompted for the CD when you try to uninstall. The reason is, these programs replace the standard versions of some important system files with custom versions, and when you uninstall the program, it needs to recopy the standard versions from the CD back to your hard disk. If you don't have the CD, you can't uninstall the program.

Removing Programs through Windows

You can remove almost all Windows-based programs through the Add or Remove Programs utility in the Control Panel. Add or Remove Programs lists all the installed programs (or at least all the removable ones) and lets you remove them one-by-one with a mouse click or two.

To access the list of installed programs:

1. Click the Start button, and then click Control Panel.
2. Click (or double-click) Add or Remove Programs. The Currently Installed Programs list appears, as in Figure 4.11. (Your list will be different than the one in Figure 4.11, of course.)
3. Click on a program. Depending on the program, two Change and Remove buttons appears (as in Figure 4.11) or a single Change/Remove button appears.
4. Click the Remove button (or the Change/Remove button).
5. Follow the prompts that appear. The process is slightly different for each program.

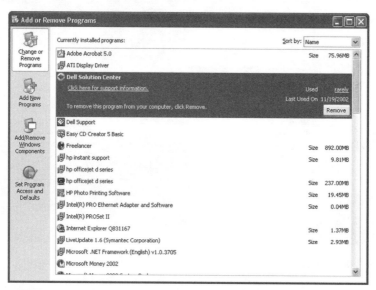

FIGURE 4.11 Select a program to remove and then click the Remove button.

Setting Up Program Shortcuts

Now that you know how to add and remove programs, take a look at a related topic—how to position shortcuts for those programs so they're convenient for you to use.

Pinning a Program to the Start Menu

You might have noticed that shortcuts to the most recently used programs appear directly above the Start button when the Start menu is open (see Figure 4.12). This is a constantly changing list, however, so you can't guarantee that a certain program will always be there.

FIGURE 4.12 The Start menu shows recently used programs at the bottom left. The "pin" area at top left remains constant.

Notice in Figure 4.12 that at the top of the Start menu there is an area that never changes. Your default e-mail program and Web browser appear there. You can *pin* additional programs to that area too, so that shortcuts to them are always available there, no matter how frequently (or infrequently) you use them.

Pin: To attach a shortcut for a program to the top-left area of the Start menu.

To pin a program to the Start menu:

1 Open the Start menu and locate the shortcut for the program.

2 Right-click the shortcut (see Figure 4.12) and choose Pin to Start Menu.

Creating a Desktop Icon

Some programs create their own shortcuts directly on the desktop when you install them. Some programs create multiple icons and even annoying extra icons that are little more than advertising. (You can get rid of these unwanted icons by dragging them to the Recycle Bin, by the way.)

But what about creating shortcut icons? Here's one way to do it:

1 Locate the program's shortcut on the Start menu.

2 Press and hold the right mouse button.

3 Drag the shortcut (with the right mouse button still held down) to the desktop, and then release the mouse button. A menu appears (see Figure 4.13).

4 Choose Copy Here or, if the option is available, Create Shortcut Here.

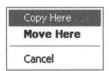

FIGURE 4.13 This menu appears when you release the mouse button after you right-drag a shortcut.

So what's the difference between Copy Here and Create Shortcut Here? If you're dragging a shortcut, there's no difference. But if you're dragging the original file (not just the shortcut to it), Copy Here makes a copy of the original while Create Shortcut Here creates a shortcut that points to the original.

Rearranging the All Programs Menu

As you install and remove programs from your PC, over time the All Programs menu (from the Start menu) might get to be quite a tangled mess. Fortunately, there are several ways to straighten it out.

The easiest way to modify the menu is to simply drag and drop items on it. To move a shortcut up or down on the menu:

① Open the menu system and point to the item you want to move.
② Press and hold the left mouse button and drag the item to another spot on the menu. A horizontal line shows you where it's going (see Figure 4.14).

FIGURE 4.14 Drag items around on the Start menu's All Programs menu to reorganize them.

③ (Optional) To move the item to a different submenu, point at the submenu name and pause until the submenu opens, and then drag onto it.
④ Release the mouse button when the item is in the desired location.

To delete an item (a shortcut or folder), right-click it and choose Delete.

But what if you want to add a new submenu to the All Programs menu? This can be useful if you want to create your own organizational system based on broad categories such as Utilities, Games, Business, and so on.

Here's how to create a new submenu:

① Right-click the Start button and choose Open All Users. A file management window opens.
② Double-click the Programs folder. The shortcut icons on the top level of the All Programs menu appear. Each of the submenus appears as a folder.

③ Right-click a blank area and choose New, Folder (see Figure 4.15). Type a name for the folder and press Enter.

④ Close the file management window. Now you can use the method from the preceding steps to populate your new menu with shortcuts.

FIGURE 4.15 Create a new folder that will serve as a submenu in the Start button's menu system.

PART II

Common Computing Tasks

5

Getting Started with the Internet

In this chapter:

◆ Choosing a Service Provider

◆ Configuring an Internet connection

◆ Surfing the Web

◆ Setting up an e-mail account

One of the primary reasons most people want a computer is to get Internet access for e-mail, Web surfing, chatting, and so on. And there's no shortage of companies who would like to help you get connected! In this chapter, I'll help you sort out your choices and set up your computer for online access.

Choosing a Service Provider

An ISP (*Internet Service Provider*) is a company that sells Internet access. You choose an ISP, and you pay them a monthly fee for Internet access. "Wait a minute," you might be thinking, "I thought the Internet was free!" Well, parts of it are free. But other parts are very expensive.

The *Internet* is basically just a big network of interconnected computers. These are not like the ordinary desktop PCs you have in your home—they're large, powerful servers. The interconnection part is free, but the companies that own these computers have to pay high fees for telecommunications lines that hook them into the network. They also have to pay a registration fee for each Internet address they use, and they have to pay technical personnel to monitor and maintain the server. That server can then provide Internet access for hundreds or even thousands of people simultaneously.

Internet: A worldwide public network of interconnected computers.

Ordinary people like you and me can't afford such a system (nor do we need it), so we pay a monthly fee to a company that *does* own one of them, and in exchange we get permission to connect to their computer and use it as an on ramp to the Internet.

When choosing an ISP, your first decision is what type of Internet connection you want. The main kinds, shown in Figure 5.1, are dial-up, cable, DSL, and satellite. The latter three are sometimes called *broadband* connections, which means they can send and receive a lot of data at once, making your overall connection speed faster and your Internet experience more pleasant.

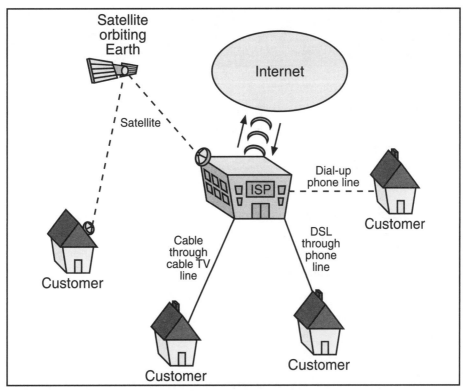

FIGURE 5.1 ISPs provide Internet access in a variety of formats.

> **Broadband:** A network connection that is capable of carrying many bits of data simultaneously, resulting in fast overall throughput.

When you buy a Dell computer, you might get an offer for a six-month free trial for an ISP. If you have no clue about what Internet provider you want, taking advantage of one of these trials can help you get your feet wet on the Internet at no risk.

Dial-Up

Dial-up is the oldest, cheapest, and slowest method of connection. It is available wherever there is telephone service, and it requires a device called a *modem*. A modem is typically a circuit board installed in your PC, but it can also be an external box that connects to your PC via a cable.

The main advantages of dial-up are its price—typically around $20 per month—and its widespread availability. The main disadvantages are its speed—infuriatingly slow—and the fact that you have to connect each time you want to use it, and then disconnect when you're finished. Dial-up also monopolizes your phone line; you can't use the phone while you're online.

If you decide on dial-up, you will have hundreds of choices of ISPs, so shop around. Don't sign up with some fly-by-night company just because they're the cheapest, though, or you might face connection problems. Dial-up ISPs can either be local companies or national ones with local dial-up numbers.

Cable

Cable Internet access comes through the same cable that your cable television uses. Cable provides fast Internet service (typically 1 Mbps or so) and does not tie up your phone line as dial-up does. It is always on, so you don't have to do anything special to connect when you want to use it. The price is higher than dial-up, but not outrageous—typically $35 to $50 per month. The main drawback is that it's not available in all areas. Check with your local cable company for availability. You will probably not have a choice of ISPs for cable because a single cable company normally services an area.

> **NOTE**
>
> Another lesser drawback is that the speed of a cable connection varies somewhat depending on the usage in your neighborhood. If everyone in your neighborhood has cable Internet access and they use it at the same time, you might experience a bit of slowdown. This is nowhere near the problem that the DSL companies would have you believe, though. (See the following section on DSL.)

DSL

DSL stands for *Digital Subscriber Line*. It works through regular phone lines, but it is much faster than dial-up (the speed is roughly equivalent to cable, around 1 Mbps), it is always on, and it doesn't tie up the phone line. The price for the lowest level of DSL is about the same as for cable, but there are many types of DSL service available, and some of them (primarily the plans for businesses) are more expensive. As with cable, DSL is not available in all areas. DSL service is available only within a certain number of feet of a telephone switching station, so most rural customers are excluded.

NOTE

Asynchronous DSL (ADSL) is the standard type offered to home users. It has a slower *upload* speed than *download* speed. Synchronous DSL (SDSL) offers the same fast speed for both uploading and downloading, but it is more expensive.

Upload: To transfer a file from your computer to another one online.

Download: To transfer a file from another computer to yours online.

DSL service comes via your phone company. In some areas you can contract directly with the phone company to be your ISP, but most people go through one of the national ISPs, such as Yahoo!, AOL, MSN, or Earthlink, for their DSL service. That company then works with the phone company to get you set up and acts as your primary contact.

Satellite

For those who need faster Internet service than dial-up, but who live in areas not served by cable or DSL, satellite is virtually the only option. It uses a specially equipped satellite dish that both transmits and receives to communicate with the ISP. A clear view of the southern sky is required. Satellite is midway between dial-up and cable/DSL in speed. Upload speed is seldom much better than a modem (56 Kbps), but download speeds average around 250 Kbps. Satellite is typically more expensive than the other options (around $70 a month), and it requires the consumer to purchase expensive equipment (around $700). The primary ISP for satellite service is DirecWay. You can order it directly from them, or you can go through EarthLink or some other ISP that has an agreement with DirecWay to provide access.

Setting Up Your Internet Connection

Most broadband Internet services offer professional installation. It's typically optional for DSL or cable and required for satellite (because of FCC regulations dealing with satellite transmitters). So if you are worried about not being able to install the service correctly, help is available! Setting up an Internet connection is actually pretty easy, though, and I'll explain how to do it in the following sections.

Setting Up a Dial-Up Connection

A dial-up connection requires a modem. Your computer might already have a modem installed, but if not, you can pick one up at your local office supply or computer store for less than $100. You can install it yourself or get a friend to help you.

Do You Already Have a Modem?

If you're not sure whether you have a modem, look on the back of your PC for a set of two telephone plug sockets, side-by-side. Figure 5.2 points out the modem on a typical Dell PC.

A single telephone-style plug that's slightly wider than normal is for a network connector—*not* a modem. Modems nearly always have two plugs—one for "in" and one for "out," so you can use a telephone on the same line as the modem.

Modems have two phone jacks on them, as you saw in Figure 5.2. One is labeled Line; connect the incoming phone line to it from the wall outlet. The other is labeled Phone; you can connect a telephone to it if you want, so that the phone line can be used normally when the modem is not operating.

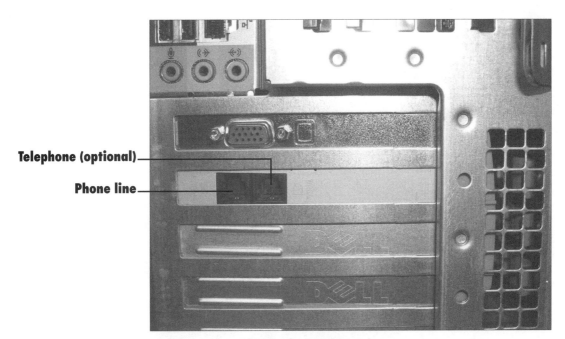

Telephone (optional)

Phone line

FIGURE 5.2 An internal modem has two phone jacks on it.

5

CAUTION

These two jacks are *not* interchangeable. If you get phone cables plugged into the wrong ones, the modem either will not work at all or will work poorly. I had a modem once that made honking noises (really!) when the modem was in use with the cables switched.

Selecting and Installing a Modem

There are two kinds of modems—internal and external. Internal modems are circuit boards that you insert in a slot inside your computer's case; external modems connect to the PC via a cable (usually USB these days). External modems are much easier to install, but they are more expensive and require space on your desk and their own separate power plug.

To install an internal modem, you will need to turn off your PC, open it up, and insert the modem into an expansion slot. Follow the instructions that came with your PC for opening the case. Many Dell computers have hinged cases that open up when you press buttons on the top and bottom, for example.

Once the PC is open, look inside for a large circuit board (the motherboard), and on it, look for white slots. These are Peripheral Connect Interface (PCI) slots, and the modem will go into one of them.

On some PCs, expansion boards such as internal modems are held into place by screws. On many Dell PCs, there is a retaining bar instead. You lift up the retaining bar to insert or remove expansion boards. See Figure 5.3. Then you simply remove the spacer behind the slot where you want to put the modem, and gently push it into the slot. Then push the retaining bar back down again and close up the case.

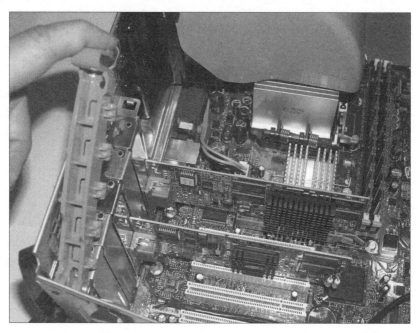

FIGURE 5.3 To install an internal modem, open the PC case and lift the retaining bar for circuit boards.

CAUTION

Handle circuit boards only by their edges, and do not handle them any more than necessary.

Then turn on your PC. Windows will probably detect the modem automatically. A message will flash onscreen about locating the new device and installing the drivers for it, and then it'll be finished. Blink and you'll miss it. In some cases you might need to run the Setup software that came with the modem for it to work correctly. See the following section to learn how to test a modem.

Testing a Modem

If you already have a modem, or if you just installed one, here's how to test it to make sure it works:

1 Click Start, and then click Control Panel.

2 Click Printers and Other Hardware. (If you're in Classic view instead of Category view, you can skip this step.)

NOTE

The Control Panel is in Category view by default (blue background); it breaks down the items into categories. Classic view has a white background and shows all items at once.

---

3 Click Phone and Modem Options. (If you're in Classic view, double-click it.) The Phone and Modem Options dialog box appears.

4 Click the Modems tab, and then click your modem to select it (see Figure 5.4). If no modems appear here, you either don't have one or it isn't installed correctly.

FIGURE 5.4 Choose the modem for which you want to view properties.

5 Click Properties. The Properties box for that modem opens.

6 Click the Diagnostics tab, and then click Query Modem.

7 Wait a few seconds while Windows talks to the modem. If the modem is working, a set of codes will be returned, as shown in Figure 5.5. If the modem is not working, an error message will appear.

8 Close all open dialog boxes.

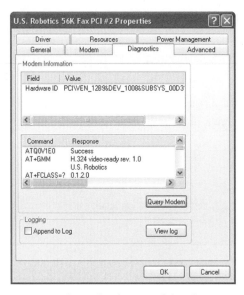

FIGURE 5.5 The results of a successful modem diagnostic test.

Creating a Dial-Up Connection

After you have ensured that you have a working modem (see the preceding section), you can create your dial-up connection. This connection will appear as an icon that you can double-click whenever you want to establish an Internet connection.

Before you get started, you will need to assemble the following information. Your ISP should be able to provide it.

- ✦ **Username and password.** These are required to identify yourself when you log on.

- ✦ **Phone number(s) to dial.** You will need these for your modem to connect to the ISP's server.

- ✦ **Incoming and outgoing mail server addresses.** These are required to send and receive e-mail using the e-mail address that your ISP provides for you.

Mail server: A computer that serves as a post office for your e-mail. It stores your incoming e-mail until you pick it up, and it forwards your outgoing e-mail to the recipient.

Armed with that information, follow these steps:

1. Choose Start > All Programs > Accessories > Communications > New Connection Wizard.
2. At the Welcome window, click Next.
3. Leave Connect to the Internet selected (see Figure 5.6) and click Next.

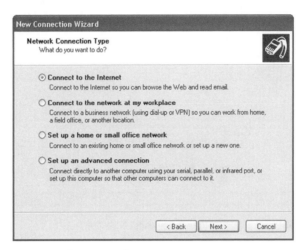

FIGURE 5.6 Create a new Internet connection.

4. Choose Set Up My Connection Manually, and then click Next.
5. Leave Connect Using a Dial-Up Modem selected, and then click Next (see Figure 5.7).

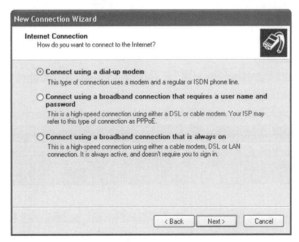

FIGURE 5.7 Choose a dial-up modem type of connection.

⑥ Type the ISP's name. This is for your own use; it will be the name for the icon. Then, click Next.

⑦ Type the ISP's phone number (the one you want your modem to dial) and click Next.

⑧ Enter your user name and password. Then, retype the password for confirmation (see Figure 5.8).

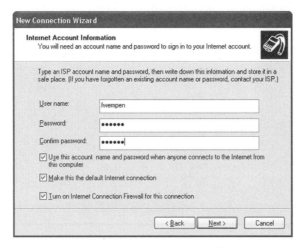

FIGURE 5.8 Enter your user name and password.

⑨ All the check boxes in Figure 5.8 are marked by default; clear any of them as needed, and then click Next. The options are as follows:

✦ **Use This Account Name and Password When Anyone Connects to the Internet from This Computer.** If you clear this check box, only the current user account will have access to the connection. Leave this marked unless the other people who use this computer have their own Internet accounts.

✦ **Make This the Default Internet Connection.** If you clear this check box, this connection will not be automatically used when an application needs Internet access. Leave this marked unless you have more than one Internet connection.

✦ **Turn on Internet Connection Firewall for This Connection.** In most cases you should leave this marked for protection against intruders.

Firewall: A software utility or hardware device designed to prevent other users on the Internet from hacking into your computer.

⑩ Mark the Add a Shortcut to This Connection to My Desktop check box, and then click Finish. Your connection is now set up, and there is now an icon on your desktop for connecting to the Internet.

Setting Up an Always-On Connection

Cable and DSL connections typically do not require any special setup in Windows. You simply connect the modem to the PC, and Windows XP automatically starts using that connection.

What about the hardware itself? Usually cable and DSL service are professionally installed or come with a self-install kit with clear instructions. A cable or DSL modem is typically a rectangular box with its own power supply.

There are three connections to be made:

◆ Connect a cable between the modem and the computer. This will either be a USB cable, in which case it simply plugs into any USB port on your computer, or an Ethernet network cable, in which case it plugs into the network interface card in your PC, if you have one. You might need to buy and install a network interface card. Figure 5.9 shows both types of connectors.

◆ If you're using a cable modem, connect the cable from the wall to the cable modem. If you're using a DSL modem, connect a phone line from the wall to the modem.

◆ Plug the power cord into the wall outlet and into the modem.

Figure 5.10 shows the connections for DSL, for example. The connections for cable are the same except you hook up to a cable TV jack instead of a phone jack.

FIGURE 5.9 USB ports (left) and an Ethernet port (right).

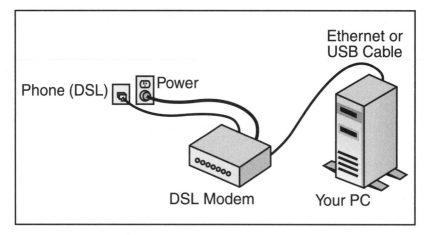

FIGURE 5.10 Connections for a DSL terminal adapter

Finally, turn everything on—first the modem, and then your computer. Windows should automatically see the new network connection and start using it for the Internet. If not, run the setup software that came with the self-install kit.

Setting Up Broadband Satellite Service

Satellite Internet service works a little differently from cable and DSL. It must be professionally installed (due to FCC regulations governing transmitters), so you will not need to worry about setting up the hardware yourself.

On the software side, your satellite ISP will give you a setup program to run on your computer. The program is fairly self-explanatory, and the professional installer will help you go through it.

Sharing an Internet Connection

One nice thing about cable and DSL Internet services is that you can share them throughout an entire household, so your entire family needs only one Internet account.

There are two ways to share an Internet connection—through Windows or with a router. Both require you to have a home network already set up, so see Chapter 10, "Setting Up a Home Network," if you need help with that. There are pros and cons to each method, described in the following sections.

Sharing through Windows

Windows XP has a feature called ICS (*Internet Connection Sharing*) that enables any computer to share its Internet connection with other computers on the local network. For example, suppose the computer in your office has Internet access, and you have a home network that connects that computer to your son's computer in the basement. ICS enables you to allow your son's computer to use your computer's Internet connection through the network.

The main drawback of ICS is that the sharing computer needs to be on all the time (or at least all the time that you need Internet access on any computer). The main advantage is that it doesn't require any special hardware besides what you've already got for your network.

To share your Internet connection, follow these steps:

❶ Choose Start > Connect To > Show All Connections.

❷ Right-click the icon for your Internet connection (see Figure 5.11) and choose Properties.

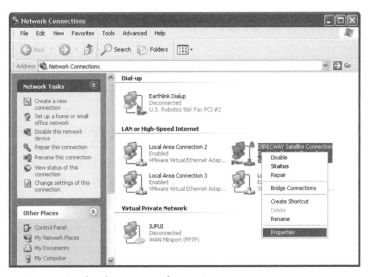

FIGURE 5.11 Display the properties for your Internet connection.

③ Click the Advanced tab, and then mark the Allow Other Network Users to Connect through This Computer's Internet Connection check box (see Figure 5.12).

④ Open the Home Networking Connection drop-down list and choose the connection to your home network (that is, the network connection that connects you to the other computers in your home or office).

⑤ Click OK. The connection is now shared.

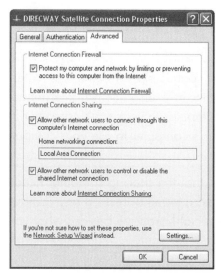

FIGURE 5.12 Share the connection with others on your network.

Sharing with a Router

A router is a networking component that reads the address on a network message and makes a decision about it, and then passes it on to the appropriate computer. Routing is a fairly complicated topic, but fortunately you don't need to know much about it for home use.

As I mentioned earlier, the main drawback of ICS is that one computer needs to be in charge, and that computer has to be on all the time. Using a router to share the connection places the sharing burden on the router rather than on any computer in particular.

Routers cost around $100 (more or less depending on the features and brand), and you can get either a wired or wireless one depending on your network. (Again, see Chapter 10 for help setting up a network.) The instructions that come with the router will help you set it up, or you can ask a techie friend for help. Figure 5.13 shows a very rough representation of the connectivity when using a router to share Internet access.

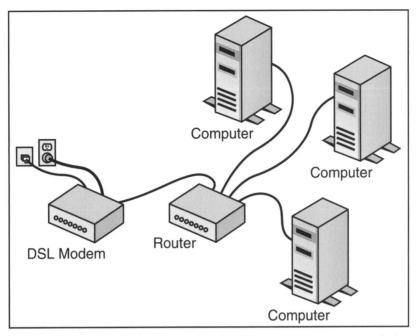

FIGURE 5.13 Use a router to share a single broadband Internet connection among multiple computers.

> **CAUTION**
>
> You cannot use a router to share a satellite Internet connection; you must use ICS. That's because the software for the satellite works on only one PC at a time.

Introducing Internet Explorer

Once you establish your Internet connection, a great way to check it is to try to access a Web page. To do this, you use a Web browser program. Internet Explorer (IE) is the Web browser that comes with Windows XP. You can use it to view *Web pages* posted by companies and individuals all over the world.

Web page: A document in HTML (*HyperText Markup Language*) format made available on a public server on the Internet.

There are several ways to start Internet Explorer. Here are three of them:

✦ Open the Start menu and click Internet Explorer at the top of the Start menu (see Figure 5.14).

FIGURE 5.14 Start Internet Explorer from its link at the top of the Start menu.

✦ Double-click the Internet Explorer icon in the Quick Launch toolbar (if displayed).

✦ Choose Start > All Programs > Internet Explorer.

When you start IE, your *home page* loads. The default home page for IE is the MSN (Microsoft Network) home page, shown in Figure 5.15.

Home page: The Web page that the browser software is configured to begin with each time you start it. The term can also refer to the top-level page of a multi-page Web site.

TIP

To change your home page, open the Tools menu in IE and choose Internet Options. Then, on the General tab, enter a new Web page address in the Home Page box.

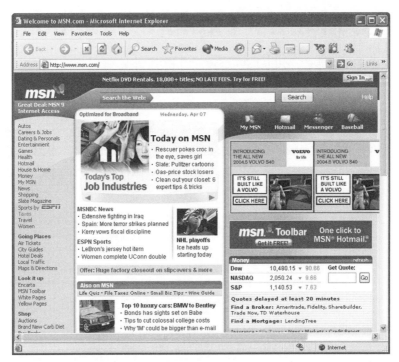

FIGURE 5.15 The default home page for IE changes every day, so your screen might look different.

Almost all of the text shown in Figure 5.15 is clickable—in other words, it's a *hyperlink*. You can click on any bit of text to jump to a Web page. On many Web sites, hyperlink text is underlined so you can readily identify it and distinguish it from normal text. However, MSN does not happen to conform to this rule, so you don't see any underlining in Figure 5.14.

Hyperlink: A bit of text or a graphic that, when clicked, opens a certain Web page, document, or e-mail window.

Pictures can also function as hyperlinks. Most of the pictures on the MSN home page are clickable. You can tell whether a picture or bit of text is a hyperlink by positioning your mouse pointer over it. If the pointer turns into a hand, the picture or text is a hyperlink.

Using the Internet Explorer Toolbar

The Internet Explorer toolbar will be an essential part of your Web surfing experience! Use the buttons shown in Table 5.1 to help you navigate.

TABLE 5.1 Internet Explorer Navigation Buttons

Button	Description
◀ Back ▼	Returns you to the previously viewed page. You can click on the down arrow to its right to open a menu of previously viewed pages.
▶ ▼	Takes you forward again after you use the Back button. If you haven't gone back, this button isn't available. If you've gone back multiple pages, the down arrow to the right will open a menu of pages to which you can go forward.
✖	Stops a page from loading. This button is not available if a page is not currently loading. This is useful when a page is taking too long and you don't want to wait any longer.
↻	Reloads the current page. This is useful when an error occurs in loading or when the page contains information that frequently changes, such as stock quotes or a counter.
⌂	Returns you to your home page.

Viewing a Specific Web Page

Web site addresses typically begin with http://. After that, many (but not all) addresses have www (which stands for *World Wide Web*). For example, you will find information about computer books at http://www.thomson.com/learning. Another name for a Web site address is *URL*.

URL (*Uniform Resource Locator*): The address of a Web page or other content on the Internet.

If you know the address of the Web site you want to view, type it in the Address text box, replacing whatever is there, and then press Enter (see Figure 5.16).

FIGURE 5.16 Enter a URL in the Address box in Internet Explorer to view that page.

TIP

As a typing shortcut, you can leave out the http:// part, and IE will assume it's there as long as the address starts with www.

Searching for Information on the Web

One of the first questions people ask when they start using the Web is, "Where's the directory? Where's the table of contents?" And the answer is, "There isn't one." Literally. There isn't one single directory that contains everything. Instead, there are hundreds—even thousands—of partial directories, each of them searchable and each of them vying for your attention. (They make their money from the advertising on the pages, so their services are free to you.)

MSN, the default home page for IE, has its own Web directory. You might have noticed the Search the Web box at the top of the page in Figure 5.15. Simply type in your search words and press Enter, and a list of matching Web sites will appear.

Here are the addresses of some of the other popular search sites:

http://www.yahoo.com

http://www.google.com

http://www.lycos.com

http://www.excite.com

http://www.metacrawler.com

http://www.dogpile.com

The resulting list from a search looks a little different depending on the search site, but they all have underlined hyperlink text you can click to visit the found Web sites, as shown in Figure 5.17. If you don't find what you want at a particular site, use the Back button to return to the list and try another address.

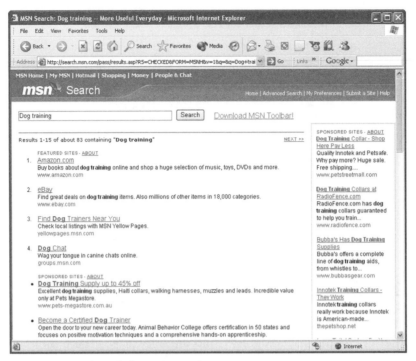

FIGURE 5.17 Search results from MSN search.

Printing a Web Page

For a quick printout of the entire page (a single copy on the default printer), click the Print button on IE's toolbar. (The icon looks like a printer.)

To access more print options, open the File menu and choose Print. Then, in the Print dialog box, select the printer, page range, and number of copies, just like you would in any other program (see Figure 5.18). Then, click Print, and the page prints.

TIP

The Options tab in the Print dialog box contains a few special-purpose printing features. If the page you are printing has multiple frames, for example, you can choose which frames to print.

FIGURE 5.18 Print a Web page.

Saving a List of Favorite Web Sites

The Favorites menu in IE stores the addresses of your favorite Web sites for easy access later. The Favorites menu comes with a few pre-created shortcuts that point to Microsoft sites, and you can easily add your own Favorites as well.

To try out the Favorites menu, open the menu, point to a category, and then click on the link to display that page.

To add your own items to the menu:

1. Display the page you want to add.
2. Open the Favorites menu and click Add to Favorites. The Add Favorite dialog box opens, and the current page's title appears in the Name text box (see Figure 5.19).
3. If you want to change the name, do so. This text will appear on your menu; changing the text will not affect the address.

FIGURE 5.19 Add the current page to the Favorites menu.

④ (Optional) To place the favorite in a submenu of the Favorites menu, click Create In. The dialog box expands, as shown in Figure 5.20. Click the folder in which you want the favorite stored, or click New Folder to create a new folder.

⑤ Click OK to add the page to your Favorites menu.

FIGURE 5.20 You can add the favorite to a submenu on the Favorites menu.

To delete an item from the Favorites menu, open the menu, right-click the item, and choose Delete from the menu that appears.

Setting Up an E-Mail Account

There are a lot of different e-mail systems out there, and it's important that you understand which type you have. They fall into these categories:

◆ **POP3.** This stands for *Post Office Protocol*. This is the kind of e-mail account you get with a regular ISP. Its mail can be read using any e-mail program, such as Outlook Express. You need to use an e-mail program in order to access it.

◆ **IMAP.** This stands for *Internet Message Access Protocol*. It's a lesser-used alternative to POP3 that makes it easier for people who travel a lot to access their e-mail from multiple locations.

◆ **HTML.** This is e-mail that doesn't require an e-mail program. You read and write e-mail from a Web site interface only. Examples are Yahoo! Mail and Hotmail. These mail accounts are usually free and are usually not connected with your ISP.

◆ **AOL.** This is an e-mail address for an America Online user. They have their own proprietary e-mail system that doesn't work with a standard e-mail program, such as Outlook Express. You have to use the AOL software or the AOL Web interface.

This chapter assumes that you have a POP3 e-mail account, because the other two types don't require any special setup.

Selecting and Starting Your E-Mail Application

Outlook Express is a natural choice for an e-mail application. It's free, it's relatively stable, and it's easy to use. If you have Microsoft Office, you probably also have Microsoft Outlook installed on your PC, and it is an even better e-mail program than Outlook Express. It has better junk mail handling capabilities, and it's integrated with some other useful tools, such as an address book, calendar, and to-do list.

A link to your default e-mail application appears at the top of the Start menu. Look back at Figure 5.14, for example—it's Outlook Express there. It might be Outlook on your system, or some other application. To start that default application, simply click its name on the Start menu.

You can also start the e-mail program from the Start menu, as you would any other program, or you can click the icon for it in the Quick Launch toolbar if it appears there.

There have been many different versions of Outlook and Outlook Express over the years, and the specific steps for each one are different. I can't cover them all here, but I'll cover the most popular and recent versions of each in the following sections.

Configuring an E-Mail Account in Outlook Express 6.0

The first time you start Outlook Express, the Internet Connection Wizard might run automatically. If that happens, skip the first two of the following steps.

To configure an e-mail account in Outlook Express:

1 Open the Tools menu and click Accounts.
2 Click the Add button, and then click Mail. The Internet Connection Wizard runs.
3 Type your name as you would like it to appear on e-mails that people receive from you (see Figure 5.21). Then, click Next.
4 Type your e-mail address in the box provided. This should be the e-mail address to which you want people to reply to your messages. Then, click Next.
5 Choose the type of mail server (POP3, HTML, or IMAP) and enter the addresses of your incoming and outgoing mail servers (see Figure 5.22). (Get this information from your e-mail provider.) Then, click Next.

FIGURE 5.21 Enter your name or nickname.

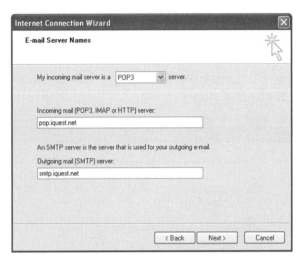

FIGURE 5.22 Enter information about the mail server(s).

⑥ Enter your user name and password in the boxes provided.

⑦ Mark or clear the Remember Password check box as desired. If you let it remember your password, you will not have to type the password each time you check your mail. However, other people might be able to check your mail if you have this option selected.

⑧ Click Next, and then click Finish. You're done.

⑨ In the Internet Accounts box, click Close.

If you have more than one e-mail account, you can repeat this procedure to set up each account. Now you're ready to send and receive e-mail.

To send e-mail in Outlook Express, click the Create Mail button on the toolbar. Fill out the form that appears, and then click the Send button.

To receive e-mail in Outlook Express, click the Send/Recv button on the toolbar. In the folder list at the left, click Inbox to see the incoming messages. Double-click a message to read it.

Configuring an E-Mail Account in Outlook 2003

As with Outlook Express, the first time you run Outlook 2003 it might launch automatically into a wizard for setting up your e-mail account. If it doesn't, follow these steps:

① Open the Tools menu and click E-Mail Accounts.

② Click Add a New E-Mail Account, and then click Next.

③ Click the appropriate server type (see Figure 5.23), and then click Next.

④ In the User Information area, enter the e-mail address and name that mail recipients should see.

⑤ Enter your logon information for the server (user name and password) in the Logon Information area.

⑥ Enter the server addresses in the Server Information area. Figure 5.24 shows the completed dialog box. (Your information will be different, of course.)

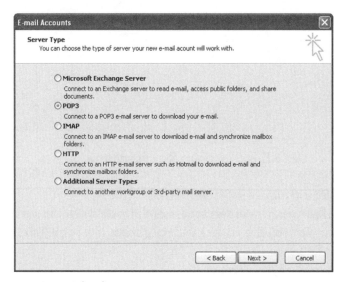

FIGURE 5.23 Select the server type.

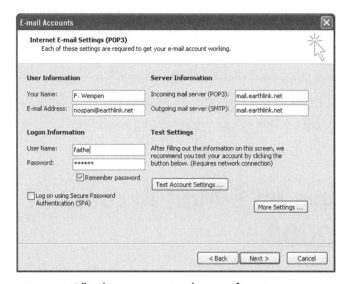

FIGURE 5.24 Fill in the user, account, and server information.

7 Click Test Account Settings. Outlook sends a sample e-mail message to your account, testing both its sending and receiving capabilities.

8 Review the test results, and then click Close.

9 Click Finish.

If you have more than one e-mail account, you can repeat this procedure to set up each account. Now you're ready to send and receive e-mail.

To send e-mail in Outlook 2003, while viewing the Inbox click the New button on the toolbar. Or, you can open the File menu and choose New, Mail Message. Fill out the form that appears and click the Send button.

To receive e-mail in Outlook 2003, click the Send/Receive button on the toolbar. In the folder list at the left, click Inbox to see the incoming messages. Double-click a message to read it.

There are many more features and options in Internet Explorer, Outlook Express, and Outlook than can be covered here in this brief overview. Explore on your own, using the Help systems in each program as a guide.

5

6

Ensuring Your Security and Privacy Online

In this chapter:

- ✦ Avoiding and removing viruses
- ✦ Screening junk e-mail
- ✦ Keeping spyware away
- ✦ Stopping pop-ups
- ✦ Filtering adult content
- ✦ Managing cookies and privacy settings

The Internet is like a big city. (Let's say it's New York City.) It's huge and colorful and diverse, and there is a lot to see and do there. But there are also crooks, credit card thieves, viruses, sex peddlers, and aggressive vendors. Do the benefits outweigh all that danger and hassle? Many people say yes. As in a city, it's all about being aware and cautious on the Internet, and in this chapter I'll show you how to protect yourself.

Avoiding and Removing Viruses

Believe it or not, there are some very scary, evil computer programmers out there in the world. They think it's fun to write programs that harm your computer and that spread themselves to other computers to do even more damage. There are many varieties of these destructive programs, including viruses, Trojan horses, and worms.

WHAT'S THE DIFFERENCE?

A *virus* is a bit of code that attaches itself to an executable file (that is, a program file). When you run that program, the virus is copied into RAM and can spread itself to other programs you run. Many viruses can also copy themselves to the startup area of a disk, so that they load into memory whenever you start the computer using that disk.

A *Trojan horse* is a program that pretends to do something useful but actually harms your computer or opens up a security hole that someone can use to view your private files or do other bad things when you don't notice it.

A *worm* is a program that spreads itself via e-mail or the Web. Some of them attach themselves to all your outgoing e-mail; others go so far as to mail themselves to everyone in your e-mail address book.

Windows XP itself does not come with any virus protection. It's absolutely essential, therefore, to install a virus protection utility on every computer that will be accessing the Internet. Fortunately, most new computers come with trial versions of antivirus software such as Symantec's Norton Antivirus or Norton Internet Security, or McAfee's VirusScan or Security Center. You choose which one you want when you order the PC, and then you get a 90-day trial of the software. If you have some other brand of computer and it didn't come with any virus protection, you can download trial versions at http://www.symantec.com (for Norton Antivirus) or http://www.mcafee.com (for McAfee VirusScan).

Virus protection programs work by comparing the contents of the files on your computer and the contents of RAM with a list of known identifier strings for various viruses called *signatures* (or *definitions*). If the program finds a match, it suspects that file of being infected, and it either quarantines or deletes it.

As you might guess, then, a virus protection program is only as good as its list of virus definitions. Those evil programmers are still out there writing new harmful programs every day, and your virus protection program can protect you against only the threats it knows about, so it's important to download new virus definitions frequently. Both Norton AntiVirus and McAfee VirusScan have automatic updating features that download and install the latest virus definitions every week.

Virus protection programs run in the background in Windows XP. When you install the program, it sets itself up to start automatically each time Windows starts, and it sits there in memory, silently monitoring every file you download, open, and save. If it sees any viruses, a box pops up to warn you and provides choices for dealing with it. You can tell that the program is running in the background by looking for its icon in the notification area (the bottom-right corner of your screen, next to the clock). To configure the program, you can double-click its icon there to open up its window (see Figure 6.1, which shows a corporate version of Norton AntiVirus).

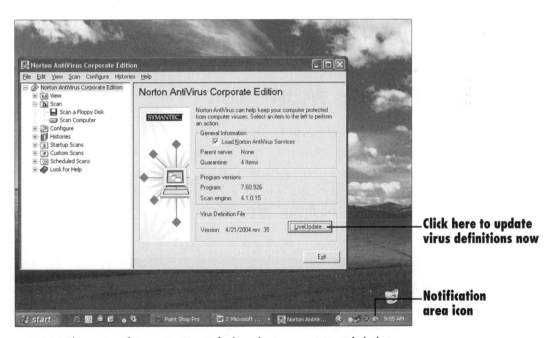

FIGURE 6.1 This version of Norton AntiVirus is for large businesses; yours might look different.

Even after you install virus protection, it is still possible for your PC to get infected, although it is much less likely. Here are some ways you can further reduce your risk:

◆ Make sure you update Windows itself regularly (as explained in Chapter 9, "Cleaning and Maintaining Your PC"). Microsoft frequently issues updates that patch security flaws.

◆ Don't open e-mail attachments from people you don't know. Even if you do know the person, first examine the attachment's name carefully. Double extensions are often a hint of a virus, such as readme.doc.exe. Also, scrutinize the message text as well; if it doesn't sound like that person, beware.

◆ Set your security settings in Internet Explorer to at least Medium. See the "Configuring Internet Explorer Security" section later in this chapter.

Dealing with Junk E-Mail

I would estimate that 95% of the e-mail I receive is some type of junk mail. It's a huge problem. Your challenge is to sort through it and delete the bad stuff as efficiently as possible while not deleting anything you want to keep. The following sections discuss some methods for minimizing the amount of junk mail you receive.

Preventing Junk Mail

The best way to deal with junk mail (*spam*) is to prevent it in the first place. To do this, keep your main e-mail address a closely guarded secret. Never enter it on any registration forms or sign-ups, and never include it in any public postings on any forums. Instead, create a free Web-based e-mail account from a service such as Yahoo! (http://www.yahoo.com) or Hotmail (http://www.hotmail.com), and use that as the address you give out to strangers.

Spam: Computer slang for junk e-mail. The name comes from a Monty Python comedy sketch in which the word spam is repeated over and over, drowning out everything else.

Identifying Scams

Some scams are obvious. Offers to refinance your mortgage, sell you prescription drugs, transfer money into your bank account, or increase the size of certain body parts are rip-offs. Don't get taken in!

There is also a much more tricky kind of e-mail scam, though. People send e-mails that look like they are from legitimate companies that many people do business with, such as eBay, PayPal, or a major banking institution. The message says something to the effect of, "Your account will be disabled unless you log in and enter your account number and password." A link is provided in the e-mail, but that link does not go to the stated company—instead, it goes to some other Web site (usually in another country) that is set up to look like the real thing. When you enter your account number and password, the person running the scam can use them to rip you off.

> **TIP**
>
> The EarthLink toolbar, which is a free download, has a ScamBlocker feature that will alert you when you have been redirected to a Web site where a known scam is being run. It's not perfect, but it helps. See http://www.earthlink.net/earthlinktoolbar/download.

When I receive an e-mail like that, I usually simply delete it. If there is any question in my mind, instead of following the link, I open a Web browser window and directly type in the company's address in the Address bar. For example, if the link supposedly goes to eBay, I type in http://www.ebay.com. That way, I am sure I'm getting the legitimate site, and not some spoofed version designed to steal my information.

Getting Removed from Junk Mail Lists

Many scam e-mails have a link you can click to be removed from their list. This is often a scam in itself, though, because if you reply to them, they know your e-mail address is good and they can sell it to other junk mail operators. Don't respond! The exception would be if you got an e-mail from a company you have a relationship with already, such as a catalog company with whom you have previously placed an order. Such companies will remove you from their lists if you request it.

The Direct Marketing Association has a "do not e-mail" list it maintains, and some companies honor it and do not send e-mail to people on the list. Go to http://www.dmaconsumers.org/consumerassistance.html to sign up. The more unscrupulous spammers pay no attention to it, though.

Filtering Your Mail

E-mail filtering is quite a difficult programming challenge because it can be difficult for a computer to separate commercial e-mail from non-commercial e-mail sent by family and friends. Spammers have gotten extremely tricky in their attempts to thwart e-mail filtering software. They will misspell words, use foreign characters, insert periods and dashes in words, put advertisements in graphic attachments, and do many other kinds of sneaky things that are hard for filters to deal with. As a result, no e-mail filtering program is perfect. There are several approaches, and each one has pros and cons.

Some e-mail applications, such as Microsoft Outlook 2003, have junk mail filtering built into them. It catches some things, but usually not all. You can also buy add-ons to popular e-mail programs (Outlook Express and Outlook, for example) that add filtering capabilities. Some of them work with a list of banned words and phrases or characteristics; others let you define what an unwanted e-mail looks like, and then compare incoming mail to your specifications. Before you spend money on one of these programs, look at reviews in magazines and consumer Web sites to find out which ones work the best. One of my favorites is Ella for Spam Control (http://www.openfieldsoftware.com).

Some service providers, such as EarthLink, offer aggressive spam filtering as part of your e-mail service. However, there are typically limitations on it. For example, with EarthLink, the filtering covers only your EarthLink e-mail address; if you have other e-mail addresses, it will not check mail coming to them. These providers also might require that you read and write e-mail through their own proprietary interface, rather than a normal generic e-mail program, such as Outlook Express.

Proxy servers can also be helpful in screening spam. I use a service called SAproxy Pro (http://www.statalabs.com), for example, that screens incoming e-mail before it hits my computer. It marks e-mail that it suspects of being spam with *****SPAM****** in the heading. I set up an e-mail handling rule in Outlook that redirects all mail with that heading to a junk folder.

The most aggressive way to combat spam is through a *whitelist*, where no e-mail gets through to you at all except from people you have specifically allowed. This works, but it also prevents you from getting e-mail from long-lost friends and other people who you might not have been expecting. Some whitelist services will send back a challenge e-mail to the sender, asking him or her to send more information so you can decide whether or not to grant the sender permission to contact you.

Whitelist: A list of e-mail addresses of people who are allowed to send you e-mail. If you use a whitelist-based e-mail filtering system, mail from anyone not on the list is blocked until the sender can be verified.

Preventing Adware and Spyware

As you are surfing the Web, innocently viewing Web pages, a box might pop up at some point, asking for permission to install some utility that it claims is needed. You have no idea what it means, so you click Yes. Then the annoying things start. Maybe you have a new toolbar in Internet Explorer that won't go away, or advertising pop-ups keep appearing, or your searches are redirected to some unexpected place, or your start page has changed. You've been hit with adware!

Adware is software that exists to display ads. You don't want it on your computer. Sometimes it hides behind claims that it provides some useful service, but that's smoke and mirrors. A related category, spyware, also claims to do something useful, but actually keeps records on your Web surfing habits and reports them back to a marketing company. Some really unscrupulous spyware makers even capture your private e-mails, user names, passwords, and credit card numbers.

You can at least partially avoid adware and spyware by following these steps:

✦ Set your Internet Explorer security settings to at least Medium. (See the "Configuring Internet Explorer Security" section later in this chapter.) This forces a confirmation box to appear before any unauthorized software can be installed as you are viewing Web sites.

✦ If a pop-up box appears when you are using the Web, asking permission to install something, choose No or Cancel.

✦ If any type of warning box appears as you are using the Web, suspect a scam. Close the box by clicking its close button in the top-right corner; don't click on any of the buttons in the window. Some unscrupulous Web site owners set up pop-ups to resemble error messages to trick you into clicking on something that will download adware.

Some adware programs can be removed through Add/Remove Programs. Go through the list of installed applications, as you learned in Chapter 4, and if you see any that you don't recognize as a program you use, remove them. (Or, to be cautious, ask a techie friend for an evaluation of whether you should remove these programs.) Also, look in the notification area for icons of programs running in the background. Some adware programs show their icons here (although the really nasty, unscrupulous ones are stealthier than that).

Your best bet, however, is to install an anti-spyware application and run it frequently. Fortunately, one of the best ones on the market today is free! It's called Spybot Search & Destroy, and you can get a copy at http://www.safer-networking.org.

Stopping Pop-Ups

Pop-ups are additional Web windows that appear automatically as you are viewing Web sites. They usually contain some kind of ad or scam. Even legitimate, big-name Web sites use them, such as Barnes & Noble's site (http://www.bn.com), but most people find them annoying.

Many utilities are available that will stop pop-ups, if you don't mind paying for them. However, recently Google, Yahoo!, MSN, and several other companies have released toolbars for Internet Explorer that will stop pop-up ads, and these toolbars are free. (The companies offering them want you to use their search engines, and the toolbars contain search boxes for their sites as well as the pop-up blocker tools.) Because they're free, you can try out several and see which one you like best.

Here are links to some of the popular ones.

- ◆ Yahoo! Companion toolbar: http://companion.yahoo.com
- ◆ MSN toolbar: http://toolbar.msn.com
- ◆ Google toolbar: http://toolbar.google.com
- ◆ EarthLink toolbar: http://www.earthlink.net/earthlinktoolbar/download

I am currently using the Google toolbar on my PC, as shown in Figure 6.2.

FIGURE 6.2 The Google toolbar shown here can block pop-ups, among its other capabilities.

Enabling or Disabling Firewall Protection

Determined computer hackers can sometimes break into a person's computer and steal their data. This is much more common for companies than for individuals, because companies are more likely to have information that hackers will find worthy of their time. However, it is still a concern for individuals as well, especially those with broadband Internet connections, such as cable or DSL.

Windows XP has a *firewall* utility built into it that can make it more difficult for someone to break into your computer over the Internet. (Notice that I said "more difficult," not "impossible.") It is enabled by default, so you do not have to do anything special to turn it on.

> **Firewall:** A program or device that prevents other users on the Internet from browsing or altering the contents of your hard drive through your Internet connection.

In some cases, having a firewall can interfere with your ability to connect to a particular Web site. This problem doesn't usually occur with publicly available sites, but it's good to know how to disable the firewall just in case. Here's how:

1. Open the Start menu and click My Network Places.
2. Under Network Tasks, click View Network Connections.
3. Right-click the icon for your Internet connection and choose Properties.
4. In the Properties box, click the Advanced tab.
5. Mark or clear the check box under Internet Connection Firewall.
6. Click OK.

Configuring Internet Explorer Security

When you are browsing the Web, you must decide how secure you want to be and balance that with how many fancy Web features you want to take advantage of. The highest security levels let you explore the Web very safely, but they also prevent you from ordering items online, viewing videos, and playing certain online games, for example.

Internet Explorer provides some basic sets of security settings that it defines as Low, Medium-Low, Medium, and High. The easiest way to configure security is to simply select one of those presets. Here's how:

① Start Internet Explorer and choose Tools > Internet Options.

② Click the Security tab.

③ Click the Internet icon. This represents the Internet in general.

④ Drag the slider up or down to adjust the security settings, as shown in Figure 6.3. If you do not see the slider, click the Default Level button to reset the settings, and the slider will appear.

⑤ Click OK.

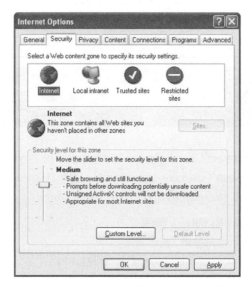

FIGURE 6.3 Drag the security level slider up or down.

If you want to get more involved with security, click the Custom Level button. This opens a dialog box with many different security permissions, and you can mark or clear the check box for each one individually.

If you want certain sites to have more or less security than others, you can add them to the Trusted Sites or Restricted Sites lists, and then set a different security level for those categories. To do so, click the Trusted Sites or Restricted Sites icon (refer to Figure 6.3), and then drag the slider up or down for that category. To edit the list of sites included in that category, click the Sites button.

Managing Cookies and Privacy Settings

Have you ever wondered how a Web site knows when you are a repeat visitor? For example, how does Amazon.com always seem to provide recommendations for books that are similar to ones you have bought before?

The secret is simple: cookies. Commerce Web sites, such as Amazon.com, place a small plain text file called a *cookie* on your hard disk. This file records your previous browsing habits and personal information, and when you revisit the Web site, their server is able to read that file and remember your settings.

Cookie: A small text file that stores information from previous visits to a certain Web site so it can remember your preferences.

Cookies are mostly harmless. Because they are plain text files, cookies cannot harbor viruses, and they cannot share your private information with any other Web site than the one that issued it. However, if you are concerned about privacy, you might choose to modify Internet Explorer's privacy settings to restrict the use of cookies partially or entirely.

To control cookie settings:

1 From Internet Explorer, choose Tools > Internet Options.

2 Click the Privacy tab.

3 Drag the slider up or down to adjust the cookie setting (see Figure 6.4). If you do not see a slider, click the Default button, and the slider will appear.

4 Click OK.

FIGURE 6.4 Change the privacy setting here to adjust how freely Internet Explorer will accept cookies.

I generally keep my cookie setting at Medium. If you set it to Medium-High or High, Internet Explorer will prompt you before writing unknown cookies to your hard disk. This might be interesting at first because you will see just how many Web sites use cookies. (Lots do!) However, it will get tedious quickly, and you will probably find yourself resetting your cookie permission to Medium.

Filtering Adult Content

You have probably read articles and heard news stories about how much sexually explicit content is out there on the Internet and how freely it can be accessed. You might have even received unwanted sexually explicit pop-ups while Web surfing. You might wonder whether there is any way to put a stop to it. Well, there is no perfect way to block all adult content, but there are some partial solutions.

Internet Explorer has a Content Advisor feature that looks for content ratings on the sites you visit and compares them to the settings you choose. For a site to be viewable on your PC, it must pass the rating test. Not all sites have ratings, so you can choose whether you want sites that have no rating to be viewable.

NOTE

There are several rating systems, and Content Advisor works with add-on programs that are available for various ones.

Here's how to set up content restrictions:

1. In Internet Explorer, choose Tools > Internet Options.
2. Click the Content tab.
3. Click the Enable button. The Content Advisor window opens.
4. On the Ratings tab, set a rating for Language, Nudity, Sex, and Violence. Click a category, and then drag the slider bar to choose an acceptable level for it. For example, in Figure 6.5 the Violence bar is set to Level 1.
5. To block or allow a certain site, type the site's address on the Approved Sites tab, and then click Always or Never to set its status.

FIGURE 6.5 Specify the limits for various types of adult content.

6

6. On the General tab, configure these settings:
    ✦ Select or deselect Users Can See Sites That Have No Rating. If this is not marked, all sites without a rating are assumed to be objectionable.
    ✦ Select or deselect Supervisor Can Type a Password to Allow Users to View Restricted Content.
    ✦ Set a password by clicking Create Password.
    ✦ Find and use some other rating systems by clicking Find Rating Systems. (Some are free; others require payment.)
7. Click OK to accept the new settings.
8. A confirmation appears; click OK. Then, click OK again to close the Internet Options box.

Now, as an experiment, try to visit some of the sites that are objectionable, to see whether Content Advisor blocks them successfully. If you need to make some changes to the settings, go back to the Content tab and click Settings. To stop using content ratings, click the Disable button on the Content tab.

7

Working with Scanners, Cameras, and Printers

In this chapter:

- ✦ Connecting and using a scanner
- ✦ Transferring photos from a digital camera
- ✦ Viewing and managing digital images in Windows
- ✦ Connecting and using a printer

Digital photography and image manipulation is no longer just for professionals! These days, everyone can enjoy working with pictures on a computer—organizing them, retouching them, and even printing out high-quality photo prints. In this chapter, I'll introduce you to the equipment you need and explain the basics of how to set it up and work with it.

Connecting a Scanner

A scanner is a copier-like device that *digitizes* pictures and text. Most scanners today use a USB interface, which makes them very easy to install. You simply plug the scanner's power supply into a wall outlet, and then connect it to the computer via a USB cable.

> **Digitize:** To convert to digital (computer) format.

Windows XP typically detects new USB devices automatically and attempts to install a driver. You can go about the next step in one of two ways:

◆ When prompted for the driver, you can click Cancel, and then insert the CD that came with the scanner and run the Setup utility on that CD. This installs the optional software as well as the necessary driver. This is the method I recommend.

◆ You can insert the CD that came with the scanner when you are prompted for a driver, and let Windows read the driver off that CD (if possible). This installs only the driver for the scanner, so that Windows itself can interact with it; it does not install any of the optional software for the scanner.

> **NOTE**
>
> Many multi-function devices are available today that work as a combination scanner, copier, and printer. Some also have faxing capabilities. If you have one of these, run the Setup software that comes with it to install all of its functionalities. A single Setup program sets up everything.

After you install the software for the scanner, you might be prompted to restart your computer. When it restarts, a background utility might load for the scanner, and an icon for it might appear in the notification area onscreen.

All new scanners made today are Windows XP compatible, but if you have an older one, it might not be. That doesn't mean you can't use the scanner if you have Windows XP, but it does mean that you can't use Windows XP's Scanner and Camera Wizard to operate it. Instead, you must use the software that came with the scanner. This is usually no big deal; I'm only telling you this because if you are in that situation, the steps in the next section will not work for you. (You will need to rely on your scanner's documentation for operation instructions.)

Here's how to tell whether your scanner is installed:

1. Open the Start menu and click Control Panel.
2. If you're not in Classic view, click Switch to Classic View. (If you see a message at the left that says Switch to Category View, you are already in Classic view.)
3. Double-click Scanners and Cameras. If an icon for your scanner appears, as shown in Figure 7.1, the scanner is installed correctly. If no icon appears, your scanner is not connected to the PC, does not have power, or is not Windows XP compatible.

For more details about your scanner, you can double-click its icon to open its Properties box.

7

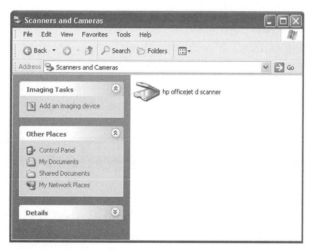

FIGURE 7.1 Look for your scanner's icon in the Scanners and Cameras window.

Scanning an Image

Unlike earlier versions, Windows XP can control a scanner using standard controls that are the same for every scanner model. This means you don't have to learn your way around new controls when you get a new scanner.

There are two ways to scan an image—you can start in an application that supports scanning, or you can start from Windows XP. If you start from an application, the scan is placed in a data file in that application. If you start from Windows itself, the scan is saved in a graphics file. Either way, you work with the same generic Windows scanner controls.

NOTE

The driver software that allows Windows to scan using a standard control set is called Windows Image Acquisition (WIA). Prior to Windows XP, there was another standard called TWAIN that many applications used for operating scanners. What's TWAIN? *Technology Without An Interesting Name*. See, who says computer geeks have no sense of humor? I'm not making that up. I swear.

Image scanning is fairly simple and straightforward, but some scanners also have text-scanning capabilities, where a page of text is scanned as an image, and then run through special software that converts it to real, editable text. This is called OCR (*Optical Character Recognition*). It produces imperfect results (99% accurate still means one word out of 100 is wrong), but it can save you some time if you have to input a lot of printed text. OCR can be done with any scanner, provided you have OCR software. However, in this chapter, you'll be doing only image scanning.

Scanning from an Application

Many applications support direct scanning, including most of the Microsoft Office 2003 applications and most graphics programs, such as Photoshop and Paint Shop Pro. In addition, your scanner might have come with a graphics program that allows direct scanning.

With direct-to-application scanning, the scanned image is placed in a data file for that application. If it's a graphics application, the scanned image becomes a graphics file all to itself. (You have to save it, of course.) If the application is not a graphics application (for example, if it is Word or Excel), the scanned image becomes an embedded object within a data file (for example, a picture embedded in a word processing document).

Applications vary in the commands they use to start scanning. In some, there is an Insert Scan button or command (or some variation of that); in others, the command is Acquire. Your best bet is to check the documentation or Help system for the individual application.

As an example, here's how the process works in Microsoft Word 2003:

❶ Start Word 2003.
❷ Choose Insert > Picture > From Scanner or Camera. A box appears asking you to choose the device—even if you have only one (see Figure 7.2).

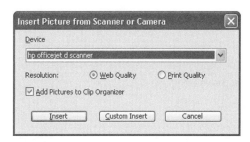

FIGURE 7.2 Select the scanner and an image quality.

❸ Choose your scanner, if it's not already selected. You probably have only one scanner, but any digital cameras that are connected to the PC also appear on this list.
❹ Choose the scan resolution. Choose Web for a low-resolution scan suitable for use online; choose Print for a high-resolution scan suitable for use in print.

CAUTION

Choosing Print will result in a much larger file that takes up more space on your hard disk.

---

❺ Click on Insert. The picture is immediately scanned and placed in the document, and you're finished.
OR
Click on Custom Insert. The Scan Using dialog box opens. (The exact name of the dialog box will depend on your scanner model.) It has the same controls as the Scanner and Camera Wizard, described in the following section.

Scanning from Windows Itself

Most applications scan by tying into Windows Image Acquisition (WIA), the generic set of scanner controls in Windows XP. In the preceding procedure, in Step 5 you had a choice of Insert, which accepts the default settings, and Custom Insert, which displays the WIA controls. Now I'll show you how to access those controls directly.

① Choose Start > All Programs > Accessories > Scanner and Camera Wizard.

② In the Welcome box, click Next. The Scanner and Camera Wizard controls appear (see Figure 7.3).

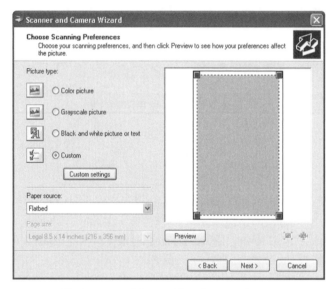

FIGURE 7.3 The Scanner and Camera Wizard settings for scanning.

③ Choose a picture type: Color, Grayscale, Black and White Picture or Text, or Custom.

> **NOTE**
>
> Grayscale scans take up less disk space than color ones, and black and white scans take up even less space than grayscale. Grayscale converts the image to 256 shades of gray, which makes the file size much smaller than when it is in color. Black and white reduces every pixel to either black or white (by rounding up or down to whichever it is closest to). This setting produces the smallest file size. It is suitable for line drawings, but a photo scanned in black and white will look like a muddy mess.

④ If you choose Custom, click the Custom Settings button to open the Properties box shown in Figure 7.4. Drag the Brightness and Contrast sliders and choose a different scan resolution, if desired.

FIGURE 7.4 Additional scanner settings are available when you click on Custom Settings.

NOTE

Scan resolution refers to how many unique pixels (dots) per inch the original image will be segmented into when it is scanned. A higher dpi (*dots per inch*) results in a larger file size, but a better-quality photo when printed. For professional-quality printing, 300 dpi is a good setting. If the picture will be used only onscreen, however, 72 dpi is a good setting because that is the resolution of a computer monitor. The default is 150 dpi, which is a middle-of-the-road setting that produces scans that would be adequate for either purpose.

---

⑤ (Optional) Click Preview. The Wizard does a test scan with your current settings and shows you the content of the scanner glass in its preview area. To change the area being scanned, drag the selection handles on the image in the preview area, as shown in Figure 7.5.

⑥ Click Next. The Picture Name and Destination box appears (see Figure 7.6).

⑦ Type a file name (no extension) in the Type a Name for This Group of Pictures text box.

NOTE

Why does it say "group" in Step 7, when it's only a single picture? Two reasons. One is that some scanners have document feeders that allow more than one image. The other is that this same set of controls is also used for digital camera image transfer, as you will see in the next section, and there are usually multiple images being transferred from a camera.

FIGURE 7.5 Drag the selection handles on the preview to change the scan area, if desired.

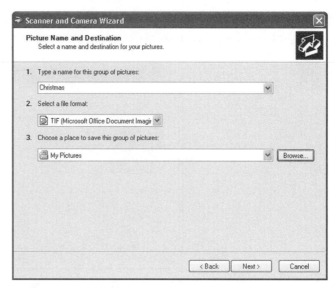

FIGURE 7.6 Specify where and how the picture will be saved.

⑧ Choose a file format from the Select a File Format list.

TIP

File formats are not all the same. For onscreen-only use, choose JPEG format (JPG). However, if you think there is any possibility that you might be using the image in a high-quality printout at some point, scan in TIF format because it is better quality (although it results in a larger file size). You can always convert the image from TIF to JPEG later, using an image editing application, or you can scan two versions—one TIF and one JPEG.

---

⑨ Choose a save location for the picture from the Choose a Place to Save This Group of Pictures list. (Click Browse to browse for a location.)

⑩ Click Next, and wait for the scan to be completed.

⑪ In the Other Options box, leave the default option (Nothing, I'm Finished Working with These Pictures) selected and click Next.

⑫ Click Finish. The location you specified in Step 9 opens in a file management window.

⑬ (Optional) To check out the scanned image, double-click on the file.

Then what? Well, you can import that image file into an application, such as Word or PowerPoint, or you can open it in an image editing program, such as Photoshop, or you can e-mail it to someone—the possibilities are nearly endless. See the "Managing Your Digital Artwork Library" section later in this chapter for more information.

Transferring Photos from a Digital Camera

You can use digital cameras with the Scanner and Camera Wizard in Windows XP, in much the same way you can use a scanner. Simply run the Scanner and Camera Wizard (Start > All Programs > Accessories > Scanner and Camera Wizard). If you have both a scanner and a digital camera connected, a box will appear, enabling you to select which device you want the wizard to work with. Choose the camera, and then simply walk through the steps. They will prompt you for a file name, folder location, and so on, and will enable you to select which photos you want and discard the rest.

However, there's a much speedier way to do this. Windows XP sees the contents of your digital camera like a mini hard disk whenever the camera is connected, and you can drag and drop images from the camera to your hard disk as easily as you can move or copy other files (see Chapter 2).

1. Connect your digital camera to your PC using a USB cable. The camera probably came with the needed cable. Check the camera documentation if you have trouble finding the USB port on the camera.
2. Turn the camera on, and set its mode to Play if necessary. (Some cameras work with Windows only if they are set to display images rather than to take them.)
3. In the Removable Disk dialog box (see Figure 7.7), click Open Folder to View Files Using Windows Explorer, and then click OK. A file management window appears.

FIGURE 7.7 Choose what to do with the pictures on the camera.

TIP

If you want to use the Scanner and Camera Wizard, choose Copy Pictures to a Folder on My Computer in Step 3 (refer to Figure 7.7).

④ If you see your pictures—great. If instead you see a folder, double-click it, and keep double-clicking the folders that appear until you drill down to where the pictures are stored.

⑤ Choose View > Thumbnails to see the pictures in Thumbnails view, as shown in Figure 7.8.

FIGURE 7.8 Windows displays the digital camera's stored pictures as files, just as if they were on a regular computer disk.

⑥ Open the My Pictures folder (Start > My Pictures). If you want to create a new folder in which to store this batch of pictures, do so, and then open it.

TIP

You can store pictures anywhere, not just in My Pictures. However, many people find it easier to always store their pictures there because it eliminates the possibility of forgetting where they put them.

⑦ Drag and drop the pictures from the camera's window to the desired location.

⑧ (Optional) Delete the pictures from the camera's window when you are finished with them.

Managing Your Digital Artwork Library

Windows XP has several useful features for working with digital images, regardless of their origin (whether they were scanned, taken with a digital camera, or downloaded or acquired from some other source). In this section, I'll take you on a tour of these features.

As I mentioned earlier, most people store their digital pictures in the My Pictures folder, simply because it's handy to do so. You can create folders within My Pictures to organize your photos. (See Chapter 2 for help with creating folders.) To access My Pictures, choose Start > My Pictures, or open My Computer (Start > My Computer), and then double-click My Pictures.

Two views are particularly useful for photos:

◆ **Thumbnails.** This view (View > Thumbnails) shows a preview of each picture as a large icon, as shown in Figure 7.8.

◆ **Filmstrip.** This view (View > Filmstrip) shows the selected picture in a large preview window, with a horizontally scrolling pane beneath the image for selecting different pictures (see Figure 7.9).

While in Filmstrip view, you can click on one of the rotation buttons below the image, or you can use the Previous and Next buttons to move between the images.

Also, notice the options in the bar at the left side of the window in Figure 7.9. From here you can:

◆ **View as a Slide Show.** See the pictures one by one in full-screen size. Press Esc to quit, or click or press a key to advance to the next slide. Press Backspace to go back.

◆ **Order Prints Online.** Open the Online Print Ordering Wizard to walk through the process of ordering prints.

◆ **Print This Picture.** Open the Photo Printing Wizard to walk through the process of printing the photo on your own printer.

◆ **Set as Desktop Background.** Set this picture in the Display Properties as the background image, as in Chapter 3.

✦ **Copy to CD.** Add the selected picture(s) to the list of files waiting to be written to a writeable CD. See Chapter 8, "Music, Movies, and Multimedia," to learn how to complete the process.

You can also do everything to the picture(s) that you can do to any other file, as you learned in Chapter 2. You can move, copy, rename, and delete them, and so on.

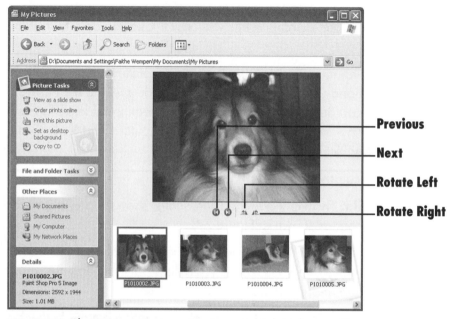

FIGURE 7.9 In Filmstrip view, you see one image at a time in large format, with the others in thumbnail format.

SELECTING A PHOTO EDITING APPLICATION

Most scanners and digital cameras come with a CD full of applications, including one or more photo editing applications. You also might have heard of other applications that edit photos. Which one is the best? It all depends on your needs and your experience level. For simple photo retouching, Jasc Paint Shop Pro is very good—and a trial version of it comes with most models of Dell desktop PCs. If you need professional-level photo editing tools (and don't mind paying several hundred dollars for them), consider Adobe Photoshop.

Working with Printers

Most people have at least one printer. In this section, I'll explain how to choose the best printer for your needs and how to set it up and keep it clean and well-maintained.

Selecting the Right Printer for Your Needs

When you go shopping for printers, be prepared for a huge array of choices! Most of them boil down to one of two basic products, though—inkjets and lasers. Table 7.1 compares the two.

TABLE 7.1 Inkjets versus Lasers

Options	Inkjet	Laser
Type of ink	Liquid ink in cartridge	Powdered toner in cartridge
Cost of printer itself	Inexpensive	Moderate to expensive
Cost of ink (per page)	Expensive	Inexpensive
Prints in color	Yes	Some models only
Speed	Varies depending on model	Varies depending on model
Type of paper	Normal, but special photo paper required for highest-quality prints	Normal
Paper feed	Single-sheet feed, typically holds 100 sheets or fewer	Single-sheet feed, typically holds 250 sheets or more, and may have multiple paper trays
Network-capable	A few models	Many models

> **NOTE**
>
> Color laser printers have been available for many years, but they have been so expensive that most people who need color have opted for inkjets instead. Recently, however, several manufacturers have introduced low-end color laser printers that cost less than $800.

Some printers have slots for the flash memory cards that store the pictures in your digital camera, so you can remove the card from the camera and insert it directly into the printer. You can also buy photo printers that don't require a computer—you hook up your camera directly to them.

When you are shopping for a printer, here are the factors to consider:

◆ **Speed.** How many pages does it produce per minute? Is speed important to you?

◆ **Quality.** How many dots per inch (dpi) does it produce at its highest setting? Do you need special paper to achieve that quality level?

◆ **Photo printing.** How well does it print photos (if that is important to you)? If possible, see a sample.

◆ **Price.** How much does this printer cost compared to other similar models?

◆ **Ink cost.** How much does an ink cartridge cost for this printer, and how many pages will you get from each cartridge? Do the math to determine the cost per page for that printer.

◆ **Brand.** Yes, it matters! Stick with a respected name brand to ensure that you will get good service and warranty coverage. You can buy Dell-brand printers when you buy your PC.

◆ **Paper.** How many sheets of paper can you put in the printer at once? How well does the printer accept odd-shaped paper, such as envelopes? If possible, see a sample and notice whether it crinkles the envelope as it prints on it.

TIP

The straighter the path of the paper through the printer, the less likely it will crinkle or damage envelopes. Paper damage and warping is usually caused by the paper winding around a series of rollers inside the printer.

Installing a Printer

Printers of yesteryear used a parallel port interface called IEEE-1284, which was also known as LPT (*Line Printer*). Look on the back of your computer, and you'll see a 25-hole D-shaped connector (two rows of holes); that's the parallel port. This port is still included on PCs for backward compatibility, but most printers these days use the USB interface instead (see Figure 7.10).

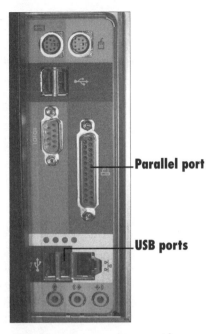

Parallel port

USB ports

FIGURE 7.10 Connect a printer to either
the parallel port or the USB port.

A USB printer is good for three reasons:

◆ USB is a fast interface.

◆ USB devices can be connected without turning off the PC.

◆ USB is fully plug-and-play, so Windows will recognize your printer
automatically without any special setup.

However, that third item is not necessarily the best thing for all printers because plug-
and-play installation does not install any of the optional software that comes with the
printer—and you might want some of that optional software! It can be useful for
maintenance and calibration on the printer, for example.

Therefore, here's the procedure I recommend for installing a new printer:

1 Unpack the printer and install its ink cartridges following the directions that came with the printer.

2 If you are installing a printer using the parallel port, turn off the computer (Start > Shut Down). This is not
necessary if you are installing a printer using the USB port.

3 Connect the printer to the computer and to an AC outlet.

4 Turn on the printer and confirm that it is working. (It should have a self-test routine you can put it through; check
the documentation.)

⑤ Turn on the PC and allow Windows to start normally. When Windows detects the new printer and prompts you for a driver, click Cancel.

⑥ After Windows has finished starting up, insert the CD that came with the printer.

⑦ Run the setup program on the CD.

If you don't have the setup CD for the printer, download a setup program from the manufacturer's Web site. If no setup program is available, restart the PC, and when Windows tries to use plug-and-play to install the driver, allow it to do so. If you have a driver disk (without a setup program) for the printer, insert it when prompted. If you don't, cancel the process, and then download a driver from the manufacturer's Web site. Then, try again.

TIP

You can also run the Add Printer Wizard. Choose Start > Printers and Faxes (or choose Printers and Faxes from the Control Panel), and in the Printers and Faxes window, click Add a Printer and work through the wizard. Windows XP has built-in drivers for several printer models, so if you don't have a driver of any kind, Windows might be able to install it anyway.

Changing the Ink or Toner Cartridge

The printer will let you know via lights or an LED panel when it needs a new cartridge. Some printers can also signal you in Windows through its driver software. Simply follow the instructions in the printer's manual to pop out the old cartridge and pop in a new one.

Cleaning a Printer

To clean the outside of a printer, wipe it with a soft, dry cloth. It is not necessary to clean the inside (usually). One exception would be if toner got spilled inside a laser printer. In a case like that, vacuum the toner up using a special vacuum designed for electronics, or gently wipe it out using a paper towel.

On an inkjet printer, sometimes the jets become clogged with dried ink, especially when the printer sits idle for weeks at a time without being used. Clogging results in poor-quality printouts with problems ranging from discolored stripes to certain colors missing entirely. To fix this problem, you must clean the jets. This doesn't involve anything physical that you do to the printer; rather, it involves running a self-cleaning routine through Windows. (You might also access this routine by pressing certain buttons on the printer.) This self-cleaning routine forces ink through the clogged jets, restoring them to their full performance. Depending on the severity of the clog, you might need to repeat this cleaning process several times. Figure 7.11 shows the cleaning utility for an HP OfficeJet D135, for example.

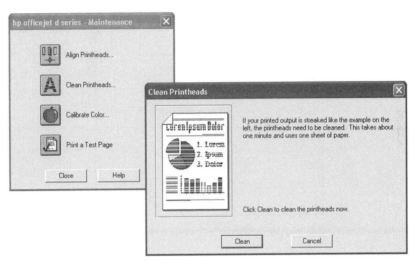

FIGURE 7.11 A typical inkjet cleaning utility.

> **NOTE**
>
> Remember earlier, when I said it was advantageous to run the full setup program when installing a printer? One reason why is that the setup program usually installs the utility you need to clean the ink jets. The process is different for different models, so check your documentation. Some models have the button for running the cleaning utility built into the printer's properties, which you'll work with in the following section.

Working with Installed Printers

To see the installed printers, open the Printers and Faxes window. You can do this by choosing Start > Printers and Faxes or by choosing Printers and Faxes from the Control Panel.

The Printers and Faxes window contains icons for all the installed printers. To see a printer's properties, right-click its icon and choose Properties. The content of the Properties box is different for different types and models of printers, but most of them have settings that control resolution and paper handling, as well as a self-test button. Figure 7.12 shows an example.

FIGURE 7.12 The Properties box for a typical printer.

Each printer has its own queue, in which documents wait to be printed. The queue allows multiple applications and even multiple users to print simultaneously; it holds each print job and sends it to the printer whenever the printer is free. To view a printer's queue, double-click its icon in the Printers and Faxes window. You can pause and restart jobs in the queue, and you can rearrange them by pausing one to let another go ahead of it in line or by changing the priority of certain jobs. (All of that is beyond the scope of this book, but you might want to try it out on your own.)

Common Printer Problems

Here are a few of the most common problems with printers and some suggestions for how you might solve them:

✦ **Paper sticks together.** Fan the paper before putting it in the paper tray. High humidity can also make the pages stick together, so run a dehumidifier in the room. You might also be able to adjust the paper thickness setting on the printer.

◆ **Regular paper jams frequently.** See the tips in the first bulleted item, and also try using a higher-quality paper. Make sure the rollers that pull the paper into the printer are rolling freely and are not jammed up with a shard of paper or with dust. Make sure there are no bits of paper inside the computer. Take it in for service if nothing else works.

◆ **Envelopes jam or curl.** Read the manual for the printer to find out whether there is a special way you need to feed envelopes into the printer. Some printers have a special exit tray in back that is used only for odd-sized or extra-thick printouts.

◆ **Print is too light (laser).** Change the toner cartridge. If that's not possible right away, take the toner cartridge out and shake it gently from side to side a few times to redistribute the toner in it.

◆ **Print is missing one color (inkjet).** Clean the ink jets. (See the "Cleaning a Printer" section earlier in this chapter.) Try a new colored ink cartridge.

◆ **Print has colored bands or stripes (inkjet).** Clean the ink jets. Try a new colored ink cartridge.

7

8

Music, Movies, and Multimedia

In this chapter:

- ✦ Choosing media player applications
- ✦ Working with the volume control
- ✦ Playing an audio CD
- ✦ Playing a DVD movie
- ✦ Downloading music and movies
- ✦ Burning CDs and DVDs

The powerful graphics and processing capabilities in modern PCs have made it possible to turn your computer into a real entertainment center, complete with music and movies. In this chapter, you'll learn about some of the most popular ways to use Windows XP for multimedia entertainment.

Working with the Volume Control

Before you start working with noisy stuff like music and videos, you should know how to adjust the volume in Windows. That way you don't blast yourself out!

If you simply want to increase or decrease the overall volume or mute or unmute it, click the speaker icon in the notification area. A volume slider appears, as shown in Figure 8.1. Drag that slider up or down, or select or clear the Mute check box.

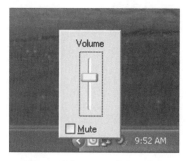

FIGURE 8.1 Click once on the speaker icon to open a very simple volume control.

TIP

Most keyboards have volume control buttons on them, along the top. You can press these to change the volume without directly accessing the controls in Windows.

If you need more control over the volume of various types of sounds, open the Volume Control window instead. There are several ways to open the Volume Control window.

◆ Double-click the speaker icon in the notification area.

◆ Choose Start > All Programs > Accessories > Entertainment > Volume Control.

◆ From the Control Panel, double-click Sounds and Audio Devices and then in the Device Volume section, click the Advanced button.

The Volume Control window has a slider for the master volume and individual sliders for various types of sounds. Drag the sliders up or down as desired (see Figure 8.2). Your Volume Control window might have more or fewer individual sliders.

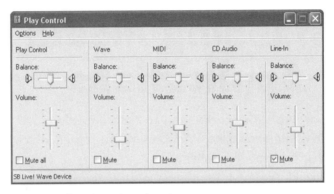

FIGURE 8.2 The Volume Control window.

8

NOTE

The individual controls work in relation to the master volume; for example, if you set the master volume to 25% and the CD Player volume to 50%, the CD player's volume will be 50% of the master volume.

Notice in Figure 8.2 that all of these volume sliders are for playback devices. There is a separate set for recording devices. To see them, choose Options > Properties, select the Recording option button, as shown in Figure 8.3, and then click OK. You can also use this same Properties box to specify which individual sliders will appear in the Volume Control window; mark or clear check boxes for the various sliders available.

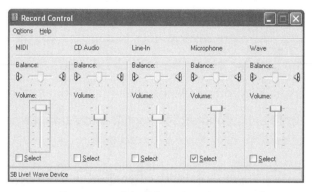

FIGURE 8.3 You can control the Volume Control properties here.

Understanding Media Player Applications

To play music and movies on your computer, you need a media player application. Windows comes with a free one called *Windows Media Player*, which you can use if you don't have another that you like better.

There are four main types of content that media players handle (although not all players can handle all types):

✦ **Audio CDs.** These are designed to be played on regular stereo equipment, but can also be played on a PC from any CD-ROM drive.

✦ **DVD movies.** These are movies designed to be played on stand-alone DVD players, but they can also be played on a PC that has a DVD drive.

✦ **Digital audio clips.** These are music clips too, but they play only on a computer (or on a specially equipped stereo system). Many different formats of digital audio clips are available, including MP3, WMA, and RA.

✦ **Digital video clips.** These are movie clips that play only on a computer. There are many formats available, including AVI, MOV, and QT.

NOTE

Some Dell PCs come with the MusicMatch Jukebox software in addition to Windows Media Player.

Depending on which model of computer you have purchased, you might have different applications preinstalled and set as the defaults for certain types of content. Some Dell PCs come with a program called DELL Jukebox Powered by MusicMatch, for example. Another popular player is RealPlayer. Some media player applications play both audio and video; others are strictly one or the other. For example, one popular video player is WinDVD, which is used to play DVD movies.

TIP

The easiest way to tell which application is the default for a certain kind of content is to simply insert an audio CD or a DVD movie, or double-click a digital audio clip, such as an MP3 file, and see what program runs it. You can change file associations through some media players' options. And although it is more cumbersome, you can also change them from any file management window (Tools > Folder Options, then make a change on the File Types tab).

At a basic level, all media player programs work the same way. When you insert an audio CD or DVD movie disc, or when you double-click on an audio or video file in a file listing, these programs kick in automatically and start playing it. They all have advanced features, too—for example, features that allow you to set up play lists and customize settings—but those features are different for every player.

Working with Windows Media Player

Let's take a look at the default player, Windows Media Player, because everyone has that one in common. Choose Start > All Programs > Windows Media Player, or double-click the Windows Media Player shortcut on the desktop. The player opens with the Media Guide tab displayed, as shown in Figure 8.4.

The Media Guide page is actually a Web page; it contains various advertisements for popular music and videos. You must be connected to the Internet for it to load properly.

Along the left side is the taskbar, consisting of names of various sections. Click a tab to display it. Your choices are the following:

✦ **Now Playing.** While you are playing a CD or a media clip, details about it appear here, including a graphic that moves to the music.

◆ **Media Guide.** This tab displays a Web page with links to media clips online (refer to Figure 8.4).

◆ **Copy from CD.** This tab contains an interface for converting CD audio tracks to digital media files on your computer.

◆ **Media Library.** This tab contains an organizer for sorting and cataloging your digital media files.

◆ **Radio Tuner.** This tab displays a list of online radio stations you can play.

◆ **Copy to CD or Device.** This tab contains an interface for writing digital audio tracks to a writeable CD or to a portable digital music device, such as an MP3 player.

◆ **Premium Services.** This tab displays links to for-pay downloadable music and video services.

◆ **Skin Chooser.** This tab contains options for customizing the way the player looks.

FIGURE 8.4 Windows Media Player, with the Media Guide page displayed.

Playing an Audio CD

To play an audio CD, simply insert it in your CD drive. If a box appears asking what you want to do, click Play Audio CD using Windows Media Player. The CD begins playing, and the Now Playing section of the player appears, as shown in Figure 8.5. You can double-click on a track in the track list (at the right) to skip to it, or you can use the player controls at the bottom of the window.

The Now Playing pane shows a graphic in the center that changes with the music. This is called a *visualization*. You can switch between the various visualizations by clicking the right and left arrow buttons below the visualization pane.

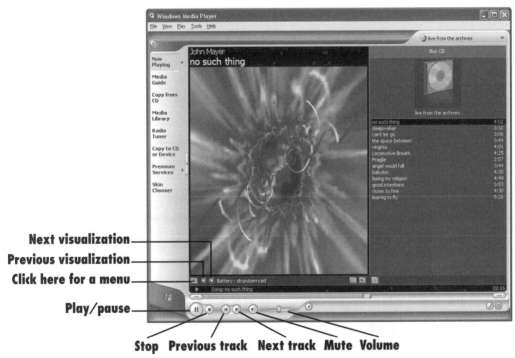

FIGURE 8.5 An audio CD playing in Windows Media Player.

There are other buttons along the bottom of the pane as well; experiment with them on your own to see what other settings you can change in the Now Playing window.

Playing a DVD Movie

Pop a DVD into your DVD drive and see what happens. The movie might begin playing automatically. On some systems, Windows Media Player is the default player for DVDs, but usually there is a separate DVD player installed, such as WinDVD.

If the DVD doesn't play, you probably don't have the needed decoder. For a DVD movie to play on a PC, you need to have an MPEG decoder installed. In the early days of DVD, this decoder was usually a separate piece of hardware, such as an extra video adapter. If you have a high-end video card, it might be built into it.

Nowadays, however, the decoder is usually a piece of software that comes preinstalled on a PC that has a DVD player and Windows XP. You also need to have the appropriate *codec* (coder/decoder) software installed for your chosen media player to play DVDs. On a new PC that comes with a DVD drive, the needed software is almost always preinstalled. Check the Dell Support site to see what's available for download if you're missing something.

Codec: A software utility that decodes the data from a compressed audio or video file. Different file formats compress and encode data in different ways, so each player must have a codec for each format it supports.

Working with Digital Media Clips

Audio CDs and DVDs technically are digital media clips, in that they are stored with numeric digits on their discs. However, for the rest of the chapter, when I talk about *media clips*, I mean computer data files that contain music or video and can be played only on a computer (or a special player that simulates a computer's abilities in that way). Digital sound clip formats include MP3, WMA, and RA, and digital video clip formats include QT, MOV, and AVI. (There are a lot of other, less popular formats too, but these are the big ones.)

In the following sections, I'll explain where these clips come from and how to play them, organize them, and burn them to CD.

Downloading Clips from the Internet

You've probably heard a lot about downloading free music clips on the Internet, and perhaps you've wondered how to do it. Is it legal? Is it safe?

Well, yes and no. There are definitely unsafe and illegal ways. By "unsafe," I mean that the methods involve sites that are likely to harm your computer with viruses, spy programs, or aggressive advertising. By "illegal," I mean that you'd be violating copyright laws, and there's a possibility you might be prosecuted. (Okay, it's not very likely, but it's possible.) I am not going to show you these kinds of methods in this book. However, there are also plenty of safe and legal ways to get sound and video clips online.

Paying for Clips

One safe and legal way to get sound and video clips online is to pay for them. On the Premium Services tab in Windows Media Player, you'll find links to several reputable services where you can search huge libraries of songs and download them to your computer for about $1 each. Don't dismiss these sites just because you have to pay a little bit! For many people, it is worth the price to have an easy-to-use, worry-free source. For-pay music sites are springing up all over the place these days, sponsored by large companies such as Apple and Sony.

Some of the music and movie download sites put restrictions on your usage of the downloads. For example, some of them require you to play the clips only on your computer; you can't transfer them to another computer, burn them to CD, or put them on a portable MP3 player. That's pretty harsh, though, and most sites are a bit more lenient than that. They accomplish these restrictions with code files called *licenses* that download to your PC along with the clip.

TIP

Without the licenses, some clips won't play. You should periodically back up your licenses; choose Tools, License Management in Windows Media Player to access the license controls.

Finding Free Clips

Another safe and legal way to get sound and video clips online is to download free clips that you find at Web sites. There are actually more than you might expect! Most popular recording artists have their own Web sites, and in many cases there are some songs you can download there. There are also large sites with clips from many different performers; for example, Artist Direct (http://www.artistdirect.com) has thousands of free clips.

Remember that Media Guide from back in Figure 8.4? Almost everything on that page is a clickable link to an article, a sound clip, or a video clip that's free for the downloading. This page has a link to an A-to-Z artist guide, as well as some featured audio and video clips. Some of these clips are *streaming*, which means they play directly from the Internet, and you can't store them on your PC for later use; others are fully downloadable.

TIP

You can store the downloaded clips anywhere you want, but I recommend the My Music folder (which is in My Documents). That way, you won't forget where you put them. If the clip opens and plays in your media player, it isn't automatically saved to your hard disk; you must go through the extra step of choosing File > Save As to put it there.

Cataloging Media Clips

Most media player applications give you the capability to catalog the clips and keep an index of them that you can choose from when you want to play them. In Windows Media Player, this index is called the *Media Library*.

The first time you visit the Media Library area of Windows Media Player, it might offer to catalog your clips for you automatically. If it doesn't, or if you want to do it again later, follow these steps:

① Choose Tools > Search for Media Files or press F3. The Add to Media Library by Searching Computer dialog box opens (see Figure 8.6).

FIGURE 8.6 Allow Windows Media Player to catalog the media clips it finds on your hard disk.

② Choose the drive to search from the Search On list. Or, if you stored your files in the My Music folder as I suggested earlier, simply choose it from here.

③ (Optional) Enter a location in the Look In box if you don't want to search the entire drive.

④ Click Search, and then wait for the search to complete. Then click OK to finish.

Now click Media Library on the task pane if you haven't already done so, and notice that all the found clips appear there, as shown in Figure 8.7. The lists in the left pane work much like the folder tree in Windows Explorer (see Chapter 2), with plus signs that expand categories and minus signs that collapse them.

> **NOTE**
>
> If you copy files to your computer from a CD using the Copy to CD feature in Windows Media Player, as described in the following section, they will automatically appear in the Media Library.

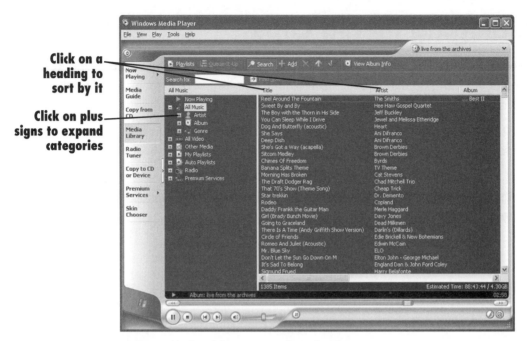

Click on a heading to sort by it

Click on plus signs to expand categories

FIGURE 8.7 The found clips appear in the Media Library.

To play a clip in the Media Library, double-click it, or click it once and then click the Play button at the bottom of the window.

Creating a Media Playlist

All media player applications have some kind of feature you can use to create a list of songs or video clips you want to play and have them play in that order. In Windows Media Player, it's called a *playlist*.

To create a new playlist, choose File > New Playlist or press Ctrl+N. Type a name for the playlist and click OK. Then, to add a clip to the playlist, perform any of the following actions:

◆ Right-click a clip in the Media Library and choose Add to Playlist. In the box that appears, select the desired playlist and click OK.

◆ Drag and drop the clip from the right pane to the playlist's name in the left pane. (The playlists appear at the bottom of the left pane, below all the artists and albums.)

◆ Click the clip in the left pane, and then click the Playlists button on the toolbar. On the menu that appears, point to Add to Playlist and then click the desired playlist name.

Then, to play the clips on a playlist, click the playlist in the left pane, so that its content appears in the right pane. Double-click the first clip in the playlist to start it playing, and the others will play automatically after it is finished.

NOTE

Placing a clip on a playlist does not remove it from the general library of clips, so you can include the same clip in more than one playlist.

One of the best uses for a playlist is to assemble the tracks that you want to put on a CD. I like to make mix CDs for my friends, and as you can see in Figure 8.8, I've created several playlists.

Playlists I have created

Content of selected playlist

FIGURE 8.8 Playlists are great for creating your own track mixes.

Copying Clips from CDs

If you own a certain CD, it is perfectly legal to make a copy of it for your own use. You can copy the tracks to your computer, and then play them any time you like, even when you don't have the CD handy. You can then copy them to a portable digital media player (such as an iPod), play them on your own PC, or burn them to a mix CD.

Here's how to copy songs from a CD in Windows Media Player:

1. Click Copy from CD.
2. Insert the CD from which you want to copy, and then clear the check boxes for any tracks you don't want to copy.
3. Click the Copy Music button. The status of each clip appears in the Status column (see Figure 8.9). When the copy is complete, the clips appear in the Media Library.

FIGURE 8.9 Copy tracks from an audio CD.

Copying Clips to a CD or Portable Player

Portable digital music players and writeable CDs have changed the way people listen to music. Now people can take their music with them everywhere they go! If you choose to create a CD, you have a choice of formats—audio or data. An audio CD will play in almost any CD player; it holds about 80 minutes of music. A data CD will play only in computers and in CD players that support MP3/WMA formats; it holds many hours of music. (The exact number of hours of music a data CD holds depends on the quality at which the music was recorded.)

Choosing Blank CDs

You'll find a lot of choices when shopping for blank CDs. Here's a quick rundown.

◆ CD-Rs are the cheapest. They can be written to only once, so if the write process has an error or you abort it, the CD is wasted. However, if you buy them in bulk, you pay less than a quarter per disc, so a wasted CD is no great tragedy. CD-Rs come in two capacities—regular (74-minute, 640MB) and high-capacity (80-minute, 700MB). They are rated for different maximum writing speeds; higher is better. Some of them are marketed as "Music CD-Rs" but any of them can be used for music.

◆ CD-RWs are rewriteable, up to 1000 times. They are more expensive than CD-Rs. I don't recommend these for making audio CDs because the technology that allows rewriting gives them a bit less contrast than CD-R discs, and this can cause problems when playing CD-RWs in an audio CD player.

◆ Writeable DVD discs are also not for audio use. You could store audio on one if you wanted to (as a data disc), but writeable DVD discs are expensive, so you will probably save them for tasks that require them, such as massive data backup. There are two formats: DVD+R and DVD-R. They are similar, but made by different, competing companies. Most writeable DVD drives produced today support both.

8

Copying Music

To copy files to a CD or portable player using Windows Media Player, follow these steps:

1 Create a playlist containing the clips you want to transfer. (If you are not sure how many clips will fit, create a playlist with a few too many; you can omit certain clips in later steps.)

> **NOTE**
>
> Creating a playlist beforehand is not absolutely necessary, but it makes it much easier to select the clips you want if you have a lot of clips. Otherwise, you will have to deselect the check boxes for all the clips you don't want from the main listing.

2 Insert a blank CD in your writeable CD drive or connect your portable digital audio device to the PC (typically via USB cable).

3 Click Copy to CD or Device. A two-pane window opens, with the current contents of your Media Library at the left and the current contents of the writeable CD or device at the right.

4 Open the drop-down list at the top of the left pane and select the desired playlist.

5 Open the drop-down list at the top of the right pane and select the portable device, or select the CD format you want.

6 In the left pane, mark or clear check boxes to fine-tune your choices of what you want on the CD. Depending on the capacity of the chosen device and the format from Step 5, some clips might not fit. This will be indicated in the Status column, as shown in Figure 8.10.

7 Click the Copy button to copy the selected files to the selected device or CD.

FIGURE 8.10 Copy tracks to a portable device or to a writeable CD.

AVOIDING THE DREADED BUFFER UNDERRUN ERROR

Because an error during the CD writing process ruins the disc, you'll want to avoid errors as much as possible. In the early days of writeable CDs, the writing process was notoriously touchy, but it's much better with modern drives.

The most common error during writing is a buffer underrun error. As a CD is written, the drive must write it at a precise, constant speed, and the computer must feed it data in a steady, constant stream. A holding area (called a *buffer*) is used to allow for any delays that might interrupt the PC from its task, but if the buffer empties and there is no data coming in at any point during the writing process, a buffer underrun will occur, and the disc will be ruined.

To avoid buffer underrun errors, do not allow your PC to do anything else while the CD is being written. That means don't use any applications, don't download from the Internet, and try to turn off as many programs running in the background as possible. Systems vary as to how strict you have to be about this in order to avoid problems, so if you don't mind possibly wasting a blank or two, do some experimenting.

8

PART III

System
Maintenance

Cleaning and Maintaining Your PC

In this chapter:

- ✦ Cleaning your computer
- ✦ Optimizing your PC's performance
- ✦ Checking for errors
- ✦ Backing up your system status
- ✦ Backing up important files

You can make your computer more reliable and easier to use by performing some housekeeping and maintenance tasks on a regular basis. In this chapter, you will learn some simple steps you can take to keep your PC clean and healthy.

Cleaning Your PC

Cleaning your PC is optional, but it makes for a more pleasant user experience, especially with the input and output components. Wouldn't you rather move a mouse with a ball that rolls easily and type on a keyboard that is free from gummy residue? And look at a monitor without a film of dust and grime on it?

The supplies needed to clean a PC are not expensive, and you probably have some of them on hand already. They include

- ◆ Soft, lint-free cotton cloths.
- ◆ Good-quality paper towels (the kind that don't shred easily).
- ◆ Denatured isopropyl alcohol.
- ◆ A can of compressed air.
- ◆ Spray cleaner or towelettes designed for computer monitors.
- ◆ Spray cleaner or towelettes designed for external computer components.
- ◆ (Optional) A small handheld vacuum designed for electronics. (Do not use a regular vacuum because the filter is not fine enough, and a regular vacuum can generate static electricity.)

You can get the first three items at your local drugstore or grocery store, and the rest at an office supply or computer store. If possible, look for a computer cleaning kit, with many of the needed products bundled together for a lower price than you could buy them separately.

Cleaning a Monitor

Always turn the monitor off before you clean it. If any liquid gets inside, it can air dry without the risk of short-circuiting. It is also much easier to see dirt and spots on the monitor when the screen is dark.

First, clean the outer casing with a spray computer-cleaning solution. Spray the cleaner on the cloth, not directly on the casing, to avoid spraying into vent holes.

Next, clean the glass using a cleaner designed specifically for monitors. This can be either a spray or a towelette. Do not use ordinary cleaning products on monitors, such as regular window cleaner containing ammonia; they can harm the antiglare coating on the glass.

Cleaning a Keyboard

Because it is always at the forefront of activity, a keyboard can get very dirty. People type with dirty hands, they eat and drink over the keyboard, they smoke around it, and so on. All this leaves dirt, oil, crumbs, and other nastiness on the keyboard.

To clean a keyboard, first turn off the PC. Then turn the keyboard upside down and shake it to remove anything loose. What falls out—and the amount of it—is often surprising!

Next, use a cloth dampened with a spray cleaning solution designed for PCs to clean all visible surfaces. Get down between the cracks with a cotton swab or a bit of folded cloth or a paper towel. I don't recommend removing keys because it can be difficult to get them back on, especially the spacebar (which has a couple of little springs behind it). If you have access to one, a small handheld vacuum cleaner designed for working with electronics can be useful in sucking debris out from under keys.

If you spill liquid on the keyboard, unplug it immediately from the PC and try shaking it upside down to release all the excess liquid and then let it dry. If the liquid was plain water or a sugar-free drink, it will probably be okay after it dries. Just clean the outside as well as possible. But if the liquid contained sugar, the keyboard might never be completely clean again.

9

TIP

Some people have successfully cleaned sticky keyboards in a dishwasher. (Yes, really!) Don't try this unless the keyboard is otherwise going to be thrown away, though, because it can ruin a keyboard just as easily as it can fix one. Wash it on the upper rack, without any heated dry cycle, and then let it air-dry for at least 72 hours before you attempt to use it.

Cleaning a Mouse or Trackball

There are many different kinds of mice available today. The two most common are a standard ball mouse and an optical mouse. A ball mouse works by rolling its internal ball on a hard surface; an optical mouse works by an LED light measuring mouse movement.

An optical mouse is sealed—and should remain that way. However, a ball-type mouse requires periodic cleaning. When there is dirt on the surface where the mouse ball is rolling, the ball picks it up and carries it inside, where it deposits on the rollers. When the rollers and sensors become encrusted with dirt, the mouse malfunctions. If the pointer jumps all over the screen or doesn't move in one direction, the first thing to suspect is dirt.

To clean a ball-type mouse, first wipe off the outside with a mild cleaner, just like you would for any external component. Then, turn the mouse on its back and rotate the plastic plate that holds the mouse ball in place. Turn the mouse over again, and the ball and plate should fall into your hand (see Figure 9.1).

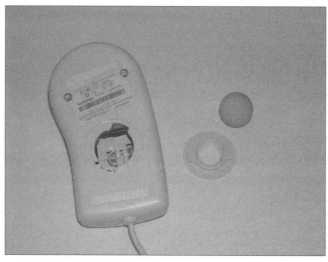

FIGURE 9.1 Disassembling a mouse for cleaning.

Clean the ball with soap and water, and then dry it with a lint-free cloth. Do not use alcohol-based products on the mouse ball because they dry out the rubber.

Next, clean the inside of the mouse with a cotton swab and alcohol, focusing on any rollers or sensors. Let the alcohol fully evaporate, and then reassemble the mouse.

If you are cleaning a trackball instead of a mouse, the procedure is basically the same. Remove the ball (you might need to remove some screws to get the ball out), and then clean inside the ball's cavity using alcohol and cotton swabs. The trackball itself is probably plastic and can be cleaned with the same cleaner you use on the outside.

Cleaning the System Unit

The outside of a system unit can be cleaned with almost any mild cleaning product, from mild sudsy dishwater to a spray cleaner in a bottle. It's only plastic (or metal), and it doesn't require any special care. Don't use anything harsh or abrasive, though.

A lot of people forget about cleaning *inside* their system units. They tend to think that the PC case is a sealed unit that no dirt can pass into, but of course that's not true. The power supply fan circulates air from the outside—complete with impurities—and those impurities settle inside the case. Over time, impressive amounts of dust can collect, especially in homes with pets, smoking, or poor overall housekeeping. Most computers will not malfunction simply from being dirty inside the case, but if there's enough dirt (think dust bunnies), it can impede the free flow of air around the chips inside, causing them to run hotter and fail faster in the long run.

You don't have to clean inside the system unit very often; once a year is about right. Here's how I clean mine:

1. Turn off the PC and take the system unit outside. (You don't want all that dust blowing around in your house!)
2. Open the case and fish out any obvious dust clumps with your fingers.
3. Spray everything liberally with a can of compressed air, blowing the dust out. Try not to touch any chips or circuit boards inside if you can help it.
4. Replace the cover and take it back inside. If the temperature and humidity was very different outside than inside, wait for it to readjust before turning it back on again.

Utilities for Optimizing Performance

Besides cleaning the hardware parts of your computer, you can also clean the software parts. Well, sort of. You can run various utilities that optimize the performance of the software by rearranging how files are stored on your hard disk, deleting unneeded files and correcting file storage errors. The following sections will show you some simple ways to make sure Windows is as tidy and error-free as possible.

Disk Defragmenter

To understand why you should defragment your disk, you have to know a little something about how the disk stores files. The storage system on a hard disk is not sequential. For example, suppose you have a text file that takes up three adjacent clusters (that is, three organizational units) on the disk. Then, you save another file, which goes next to it. Then, you add two more paragraphs to your original text file. Where are those paragraphs going to be saved on the disk? Not adjacent to the original file—that space is taken. They are saved somewhere else, and boom, the file is *fragmented*. Over time, the pieces of a file get spread out all over the place.

Fragmented: Not stored in one contiguous location.

The PC takes longer to open a fragmented file than an unfragmented one because the read/write head has to hop around picking up the pieces. Therefore, defragmenting can improve performance. Defragmenting involves running a utility that rearranges the files on the disk so that as many files as possible are unfragmented.

To defragment in Windows XP, do the following:

1. Choose Start > All Programs > Accessories > System Tools > Disk Defragmenter. Alternatively, you can open My Computer, right-click the drive and choose Properties, and then click Defragment Now on the Tools tab.
2. Click a drive (if more than one appears on the list), and then click Analyze. After a few minutes, a recommendation will appear (see Figure 9.2).

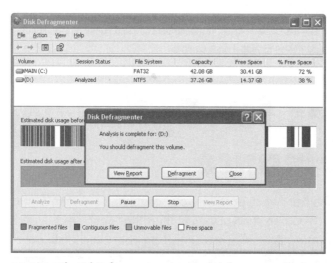

FIGURE 9.2 The Disk Defragmenter recommends defragmenting this drive.

③ If defragmenting is recommended, click the Defragment button. (If not, click Close, and then either analyze a different drive or close the application.)

④ Wait for the defragmentation to finish. It could take an hour or more depending on the drive size.

⑤ When a message appears saying that defragmentation is finished, click OK. Then, close the application.

TIP

How often should you defragment? It depends on your usage. Try it once a month or so, but use the Analyze feature to check whether or not your system needs it.

Disk Cleanup

In addition to the important files on your computer, there are probably many useless ones that could be deleted without creating any problems—if only you could locate and identify them!

The Disk Cleanup utility helps with this task. It looks at the files on your system and suggests files to delete in several categories, including temporary files, saved and offline Web pages, downloaded program files, and the contents of the Recycle Bin.

To use Disk Cleanup, follow these steps:

① Choose Start > All Programs > Accessories > System Tools > Disk Cleanup.

② Choose the drive to clean up and click OK. Disk Cleanup analyzes that drive's contents, and a results box appears, as shown in Figure 9.3.

FIGURE 9.3 Clean up unwanted files on your hard disk.

3 Mark or clear the check boxes next to each category of files, as desired.

NOTE

To see a complete list of files in a category, select the category and click View Files.

---

4 Click OK. A confirmation message appears.

5 Click Yes. Disk Cleanup removes the specified files and the application closes.

Check Disk

The file system on a computer is a complex system of pointers from one cluster to another, with a table of contents called a *Master File Table* (or *File Allocation Table*) holding it all together. Sometimes errors can crop up in this organizational system, creating a *logical error*. Disks can also have *physical errors*, which are bad spots on the disk from which the data cannot be read.

Logical error: An error on a disk that is caused by a filing problem rather than a physical defect.

Physical error: A physical defect on the disk surface that causes whatever is stored in that spot to be unreadable.

Windows XP has a utility called Check Disk that can find and fix both kinds of errors. It doesn't always fix all the errors, but it does its best. It can't repair a physical defect on the disk surface, for example, but it can sometimes read the data out of the defective spot and relocate it somewhere else.

Check Disk can be run in two modes—logical only, or both physical and logical. The latter takes much longer, so most people use it only when they suspect a problem, and not for routine check-ups.

To run Check Disk:

1 Choose Start > My Computer.

2 Right-click the disk you want to check and choose Properties.

3 Click the Tools tab, and then click Check Now. The Check Disk window appears (see Figure 9.4).

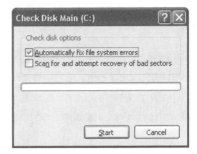

FIGURE 9.4 Check Disk helps you find errors in your hard disk's file system.

④ Select the Automatically Fix File System Errors check box to avoid having to deal with the errors it finds.

⑤ (Optional) If you want the physical check, select the Scan for and Attempt Recovery of Bad Sectors check box.

⑥ Click Start.

⑦ Wait while the check is running. A logical test takes only a few minutes; a physical and logical test can take several hours.

TIP

If you see a message that the disk check cannot be performed because exclusive use of the drive could not be obtained, click Yes to allow it to run the next time you start your PC, and then restart your PC.

If you allow Windows to correct errors automatically (Step 4), you don't need to monitor the process; simply come back later when it's finished and view the results.

9

Backing Up Important Information

Better safe than sorry, as the old adage goes. In this section, you'll learn about a couple of utilities you can use as insurance against system crashes and other problems that could potentially disable your PC or cause you to lose your data files.

System Restore

Windows is a fully customizable operating system, and almost everything you see onscreen can be altered. You can also add and remove applications, specify default devices, and much more. All of your preferences and settings, as well as all the information about the system state (such as installed applications), are stored in a big database called the *Registry*.

Every time you install a new application, the setup program alters the Registry. Sometimes, however, the new application isn't written very well, and its setup utility harms the Registry, causing Windows not to work well anymore. At that point, you would like to have a backup of the Registry as it was before that setup did its damage, right? That's what System Restore is all about—it makes Registry backups.

NOTE

There are many other ways that the Registry can get messed up besides when you are installing new software. That's just the most common way. Improper shutdown can also cause problems, for example.

The System Restore utility makes a backup of the Registry every day, without any user intervention. That way—worse case scenario—you can always go back to the previous day's Registry. It also creates a restore point before it installs any of the Windows Updates that it automatically downloads from Microsoft. You can also create new backups, called *restore points* or *snapshots*, any time you want. Then, if a problem occurs, you can use System Restore to restore the Registry to its earlier version.

Creating a Restore Point

To create a System Restore snapshot, follow these steps:

1. Choose Start > All Programs > Accessories > System Tools > System Restore.
2. In the Welcome box that appears, click Create a Restore Point, and then click Next.
3. Type a description for the restore point (see Figure 9.5). This can be anything that will help jog your memory. For example, if you are creating a restore point as a precaution before you install a certain new program, you might call it Before Install. Then click Create.
4. Click Close to close the utility.

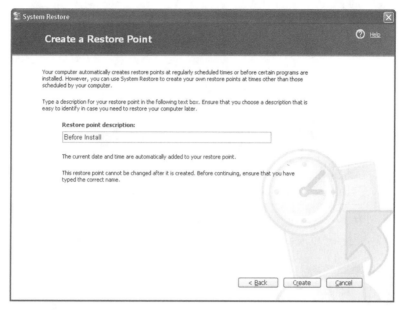

FIGURE 9.5 Create a restore point as insurance against problems when you are installing new software.

Restoring a Previous Windows State

If your system is starting to have problems, such as error messages, the inability to start normally, or lockups, and you just installed some new program or changed a system setting, you are probably wishing you had never done it! System Restore can help you go back in time, restoring the Registry to the condition it was in before the unfortunate incident.

To restore from System Restore, follow these steps:

1. Close all open programs, and then choose Start > All Programs > Accessories > System Tools > System Restore.
2. Leave Restore My Computer to an Earlier Time selected, and click Next.
3. On the calendar that appears, click the date of the restore point you want to use. Dates containing restore points appear in boldface. Some dates have more than one restore point, as shown in Figure 9.6.
4. On the list to the right of the calendar, click the restore point you want. Then, click Next.
5. A confirmation appears; click Next.
6. Your PC restarts itself. When Windows comes back up, a confirmation box appears; click OK to close it.

Your system is now restored to the chosen configuration. If that solved your problem, great. If it introduced even more problems, you can always reverse the System Restore process. To do so, restart System Restore and choose Undo My Last Restoration.

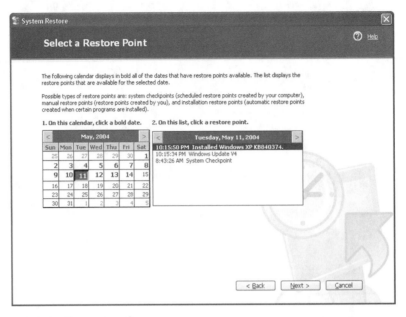

FIGURE 9.6 Choose a snapshot to restore.

Backing Up Data

Most people are more worried about their data files being safe than anything else. If Windows crashed and you lost everything on your hard disk, you could reinstall Windows and your applications, but all your word processing files and other data would be gone forever—and that would be a big problem.

You must back up your data regularly to make sure such a tragedy doesn't happen to you. There are three ways of making a backup:

◆ **Copy files to another disk.** This is the simplest method. Drag and drop the files to another disk. If you ever need them again, drag and drop them back again. You can use a floppy, a ZIP disk, a writeable CD, another hard disk, or even a network drive.

◆ **Use a backup program.** Backup programs work with ordinary drives or with tape drives; they back up a whole list of files at once from different locations, and they compress them to save space. When you need a backed-up file, you must run the same backup program again to restore it.

◆ **Mirror the drive.** You can make an exact copy of the entire hard drive onto a hard drive that is the same size or larger. This requires a utility such as Norton Ghost or DriveCopy, neither of which come with Windows.

Personally, I do not use the latter method because I find it to be overkill for my needs. I never back up program files because I have the CDs for them and I could reinstall them if needed. And I never back up anything I have downloaded because I could download it again. I mostly use a plain old copy operation for backing up my data files. However, Microsoft Backup is very good too.

Installing Microsoft Backup in Windows XP Home Edition

Microsoft Backup comes preinstalled with Windows XP Professional. It also comes with Windows XP Home Edition, but it is not preinstalled so you must install it from your Windows XP Home Edition CD-ROM.

Dell computers that have Windows XP preinstalled come with an Operating System Reinstallation CD. Here's how to install Microsoft Backup from such a CD:

1. Insert the CD in your CD drive. In the Welcome to Windows XP window, click Perform Additional Tasks.
2. Click Browse This CD.
3. Navigate to the \VALUEADD\MSFT\NTBACKUP folder on the CD.
3. Double-click Ntbackup.msi.
4. Follow the prompts.

Backing Up Documents and Settings Using Microsoft Backup

To run Microsoft Backup, choose Start > All Programs > Accessories > System Tools > Backup. (If it's not there, see the preceding section.)

Microsoft Backup runs in Wizard mode by default; you simply follow the prompts to back up or restore. There are advanced modes from which you can select exactly what files to back up, but this book covers only the simple method.

To back up your documents and settings (assuming your documents are stored in the My Documents folder), follow these steps:

1. Choose Start > All Programs > Accessories > System Tools > Backup. The Backup or Restore Wizard runs. Click Next to begin.
2. Click Back Up Files and Settings, and then click Next.
3. Click My Documents and Settings, and then click Next.
4. In the Choose a Place to Save Your Backup box, enter the path to the desired location. (You can click Browse to locate it, if you want.) If you are backing up to a drive, type the drive letter here.

9

⑤ In the Type a Name for This Backup box, type a name for the backup file set. Then, click Next.

⑥ Click Finish. Then wait for the backup to complete. The Backup Progress box appears as the backup is occurring (see Figure 9.7).

⑦ When the Backup Progress box reports that backup is complete, click Close.

FIGURE 9.7 This box shows the progress of the backup.

This method I showed you is simple, but there are also advanced options and settings that give you more control; experiment with these on your own if you're interested. For example, you can select which files to back up, which is useful if you store your data files in some location other than My Documents.

Restoring from a Microsoft Backup Set

If you ever need to restore your backup, you will first want to bring the PC up to an operational state if something is wrong with it. That might mean reloading Windows. When everything seems to be working okay, use these steps to restore your backup:

1. Choose Start > All Programs > Accessories > System Tools > Backup. The Backup or Restore Wizard runs. Click Next to begin.
2. Click Restore Files and Settings, and then click Next.
3. Double-click an item on the left to see its contents, and then select the check box for the folder/drive you want to restore. Then click Next.
4. Click Finish. The restore process begins.
5. When the restore is complete, click Close.

Downloading and Installing Windows Updates

Microsoft frequently updates Windows by offering bug fixes and security patches. Windows has an AutoUpdate feature that automatically checks the Microsoft servers and downloads all critical updates. You can also access Microsoft Update manually to check for non-critical updates.

Using AutoUpdate

Shortly after you install Windows (or start using a new PC with it preinstalled), an icon will appear in the notification area (to the left of the clock) with a blurb over it that says "Stay Current with Automatic Updates." Click on it, and it will walk you through a one-time setup process via an Automatic Updates Setup Wizard. Just follow the prompts.

Your choices in this Setup Wizard are the following:

- ◆ **Download the Updates Automatically and Notify Me When They Are Ready to be Installed.** This is the default option. The updates are downloaded, but you must give your permission each time for their installation. This option is good for systems with high-speed, always-on Internet connections.

- ◆ **Notify Me before Downloading Any Updates and Notify Me Again before Installing Them on My Computer.** With this option, you choose when updates are downloaded as well as installed. This can be useful if you don't want downloads interfering with your Internet speed on a slow connection.

- ◆ **Turn Off Automatic Updating. I Want to Update My Computer Manually.** Choose this option if you don't want AutoUpdate. If you do this, you will need to use Windows Update as described later in the chapter.

After you have configured AutoUpdate initially, the AutoUpdate icon will reappear in the notification area whenever an update is available. At that point you can ignore the icon until it's convenient to deal with it, or you can double-click it to begin the installation. Figure 9.8 shows an Automatic Update that is ready to install. You can click Details if you are curious about what it is, but you should always install the update.

FIGURE 9.8 An Automatic Update is downloaded and ready for installation.

TIP

Some of the updates require you to restart your PC afterwards; others don't. Sometimes if you click Details, it will tell you whether the current update will require a restart. This is useful to know because you might postpone the installation if you are in the middle of something in another application and you don't want to restart right away.

Manually Updating Windows

If you choose not to use AutoUpdate, you will need to check for updates manually with Windows Update. You might also want to periodically check for updates manually to get any optional updates because these do not show up with AutoUpdate. Optional updates might include a new version of Windows Media Player or a new driver for your video card, for example.

To start Windows Update, choose Start > All Programs > Windows Update, or open your Web browser and go to http://v4.windowsupdate.microsoft.com/en/default.asp.

Internet Explorer opens and connects to the Internet, and a Windows Update page displays. The first time you visit this page, you might be prompted to download and install an ActiveX control from Microsoft; if prompted you must do this or you can't continue.

From that point, simply follow the prompts. Click Scan for Updates, and then review and install the updates it finds. You should install all critical updates plus any of the other updates that seem like they would be useful for your situation (see Figure 9.9).

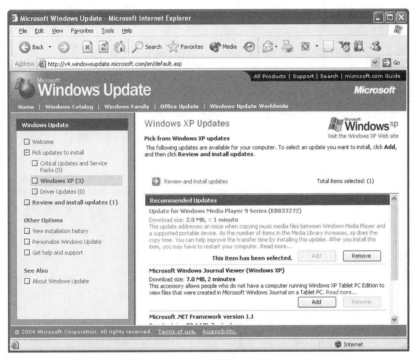

FIGURE 9.9 Install the updates that Windows Update finds for your computer.

10

Setting Up a Home Network

In this chapter:

- ✦ What is a network?
- ✦ Wired or wireless?
- ✦ What you will need
- ✦ Installing networking components
- ✦ Setting up a Windows network
- ✦ Using a Windows network

As computers become more and more affordable, many homes are ending up with two, three, or even more of them. In the olden days, people who wanted to share data between computers would carry the data on a floppy disk; this used to be jokingly called "sneaker-net." Today, though, there are a variety of inexpensive ways to connect the PCs in your home to share data, printers, and even Internet connectivity.

What Is a Network?

In its simplest form, a *network* is two or more computers that are connected in some way. There are all sizes of networks, from two computers all the way up to the entire Internet, with millions of users. Possible connection methods include cables, phone lines, electrical conduit, infrared light, and radio waves.

There are two main types of networks: those with a dedicated *server* and those without one. On a server-based network, all the data passes through the server on the way to its final destination. The server acts as a traffic cop, and in many cases it also serves as a repository for shared data. The PCs that use the services of the server are called *clients*.

Server: A computer that provides services to other computers on a network rather than doing anything directly for a human user.

A network without a server is called a *peer-to-peer* (P2P) network. Because there is no server, all must share in the networking burden. This usually is not a problem because the burden is very light, but the burden increases with each computer added to the network and finally becomes unwieldy at about 10 computers. Because most home networks have fewer than 10 computers, and because they typically don't have a spare computer available to serve as a server, almost all home networks are peer to peer.

Peer to peer: A type of network where there is no server to manage the network, so each of the client computers shares equally in the burden of maintaining the network.

Network Technologies

Browsing the networking section at the Dell online accessories store, or your local electronics retailer, will show you several networking possibilities for small peer-to-peer networks.

Standard Ethernet

The traditional type of networking is *Ethernet*, which is also the type used for most client/server networks. Each PC must have a network adapter, and there must be a *hub*, which is a small box that serves as a physical gathering point for all network traffic. Each PC's network adapter connects to the hub via a cable. It is fast, reliable, and inexpensive. However, you have to run network cables all over your house to use it.

Power Line or Phone Line Networking

Don't want to run those cables? You can buy networking kits for networks that connect through the telephone jacks in your home or through the electrical outlets. These networks work well in buildings where the computers are physically far apart, perhaps on separate floors. You need different equipment for this type of network than what's pictured and described in this chapter; however, this type of networking is sold mostly in kits with clear instructions, so you should not have to make any difficult decisions with it.

> **NOTE**
>
> This business of running network signals through the power lines seems poised for the big time. A major electric company has just announced that it plans to offer broadband Internet service to its customers through power lines within the next year or so.

10

Wireless Networking

Wireless networking is the really hot home network technology right now. It is very much like traditional Ethernet networking (and compatible with it) except that it uses a different conduit than normal—radio waves. You can even combine a wired network with a wireless one, serving some PCs one way and others another way.

Why isn't everyone running out and buying wireless networking equipment? In fact, a lot of people are. But those who aren't have these reasons:

◆ **It's more expensive.** You'll pay twice (or more) as much for wireless equipment as for wired.

◆ **The standards are still evolving.** There are three standards for equipment you'll see on the market today: 802.11a, 802.11b, and 802.11g. The "b" version was the first and most popular, and the "g" version is an updated version of it and backward compatible with it. The "a" version, on the other hand, is different and incompatible with both of the others.

◆ **It's less secure.** The radio waves go blasting out in all directions from your house, and anyone in the neighborhood can hook into your network unless you implement some type of security. Most wireless equipment has optional security you can enable, but some beginners may not think to do it.

◆ **The signal fades with distance.** As you move farther away from the wireless access point, the signal begins to degrade, and you may experience connectivity problems. A single wireless access point can serve an entire house if you position the access point near the center, but if you have several floors to go through or exceptionally thick walls and floors (such as in an historic home), you probably won't be able to access an access point from the attic while you're in the basement.

I don't want to scare you off of wireless networking, because personally I find it very useful, and I have a wireless network in my own home. I just don't want you to think it's a panacea.

What You Will Need

Don't panic—the equipment you need for networking is not expensive, and you may even already have some of it. You will need a network adapter for each PC, an access point or hub, and some cables to connect it all together (unless you're building a wireless network, of course).

Network Adapters

A *network adapter* is a device that helps the PC send data to the network. It is sometimes called a network interface card (NIC), although these days there are other types besides cards (such as circuit boards).

Each PC will need its own network adapter. Nearly all Dell PCs sold today come with built-in Ethernet adapters, so you probably do not need to buy one. Look on the back of your PC for a plug that looks like it might take a phone connector but is a little bit too wide and that has a small green LED next to it. That's an Ethernet connector. See Figure 10.1.

Ethernet connector

FIGURE 10.1 Look for an Ethernet port on the back of your computer.

10

If you don't have a network adapter already, or if you have a wired one (as shown in Figure 10.1) but want a wireless network, you will need to buy a network adapter—a separate one for every PC that doesn't already have one.

The network adapter can be either a circuit board you install in the PC or a USB device you plug into one of the PC's external USB ports. For notebook PCs, it can be a PC card device. Figure 10.2 shows some wired models, and Figure 10.3 shows wireless ones.

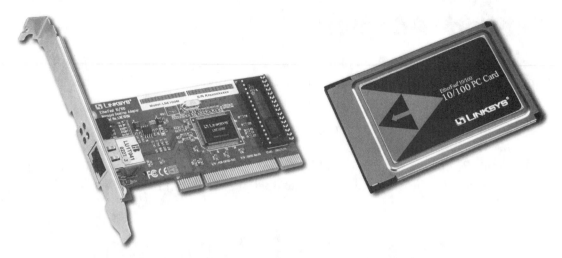

FIGURE 10.2 Wired network adapters (courtesy of Linksys).

FIGURE 10.3 Several types of wireless network adapters (courtesy of Linksys).

After deciding on the physical form you want, next consider the standard it should support.

If it will be a wired network, look for network adapters that are 100BaseT or 10/100BaseT. Bypass the Gigabit Ethernet models, as they're expensive and faster than you will need.

For a wireless network, look for 802.11b or 802.11g. The b version will be cheaper and operates at 10Mbps; the g version operates at 100Mbps and is backward compatible with b equipment. Avoid the 802.11a models; a is a separate and incompatible standard.

Network Hub or Access Point

You also will need a box that will serve as the central gathering point for the network. For a wired network, this box is called a *hub*. It has ports into which you can plug cables that run from each network adapter. See Figure 10.4.

FIGURE 10.4 A small hub for a wired network (courtesy of Linksys).

For a wireless network, it's an *access point*, which is just like a hub except that it handles wireless Ethernet instead of wired. Instead of ports, it has antennae. Some access points also include a few regular ports so that you can join a wired network and a wireless one together (or so that some PCs can connect as wired and others as wireless). See Figure 10.5.

FIGURE 10.5 A wireless access point (Courtesy of Linksys).

TIP

If the primary reason for networking the PCs is to share Internet access, you might consider a router (or wireless router) instead of a hub or access point. The access point shown in Figure 10.5 has both access point and router functionality. Make sure you read the section "Sharing an Internet Connection" later in this chapter before making your purchase.

Installing Networking Components

First, you install the network adapters in the individual PCs. Then you connect them all together via the hub or access point.

Installing a Network Adapter

Installing a network adapter is easy—especially if you have a USB or PC card type. (And even the circuit board type is not *that* difficult.) Read the directions that came with your network adapter. That will be a much better source of specific information about your model than this book can be. In fact, you can just set this book down at this point and follow those directions.

Installing a USB or PC Card Network Adapter

Both of these types are plug-and-play, and both can be plugged in with the computer running. A USB model plugs into a USB port (naturally!), and a PC card model plugs into the PC card slot on a notebook PC.

Windows will immediately notice the new hardware and prompt you for a driver. Insert the CD that came with the adapter and follow the prompts. Easy stuff! If you have problems with this method, click Cancel and then run the setup program on the adapter's CD.

Installing a Circuit Board Network Adapter

Installing a circuit board in a PC is not difficult, so don't let it intimidate you! It's exactly the same as installing a modem, which I covered in Chapter 5, so flip back there if you need help. The network adapter itself will also probably have good instructions included in its box.

Installing and Connecting a Hub or Access Point

The hub or access point is separate from the PC. It has its own power supply and can even sit in a different room if you like. Just plug it into an AC outlet.

If it's a wired network, run a cable from the PC's network adapter to one of the ports on the back of the hub. On the back of a hub you'll see a row of numbered plugs, as in Figure 10.6. Plug any cable into any of the numbered plugs. However, avoid the special plug that's off by itself and labeled Uplink or Internet. This is a special purpose slot for connecting this hub with other hubs or with a router, and it's not suitable for connecting one of the individual PCs.

If it's a wireless network with no cables, just plug it in and turn it on, and you're good to go. There may be an optional configuration utility you can run; check the documentation to find out.

10

FIGURE 10.6 Connect cables to the back of a hub.

Setting Up a Network in Windows

There are two steps to setting up a home network:

◆ Making Windows see your network adapter.

◆ Making Windows use it to communicate with the other computers.

Checking the Network Adapter

Here's how to tell if your network adapter is installed:

① In the Control Panel (Classic view), double-click System.

② Click the Hardware tab, and then click Device Manager.

③ In the list of devices, click the plus sign next to Network Adapters (see Figure 10.7).

④ Do one of the following:

    a.   If it appears on the list with no special symbols next to it (such as an exclamation point or a red X), it's installed; close Device Manager.

b. If you don't see your network adapter on that list or if there is no Network Adapters category on the list, then Windows doesn't see it. Try reinstalling it.

c. If it appears on the list but with a yellow circle and exclamation point next to it, there's a problem with it. Try reinstalling it, and try reinstalling the setup software that came with it.

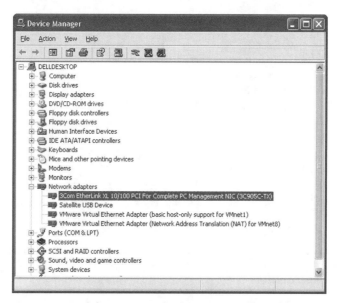

FIGURE 10.7 Look for your network adapter in Device Manager to confirm that it is working.

Running the Network Setup Wizard

The Network Setup Wizard installs the needed network drivers and *protocols*, it configures your computer for Internet connection sharing if desired, and it enables file and printer sharing.

10

> **Protocol:** A language that a network component uses to speak to other components. The most popular one is TCP/IP, which is also the protocol used on the Internet.

To run the Network Setup Wizard:

❶ Choose Start > All Programs > Accessories > Communications > Network Setup Wizard.

❷ Click Next to begin.

❸ Read the information, and confirm that you have taken all the listed pre-steps; then click Next.

④ On the Select a Connection Method screen, choose the statement that best matches your computer's situation. See Figure 10.8. Then click Next.

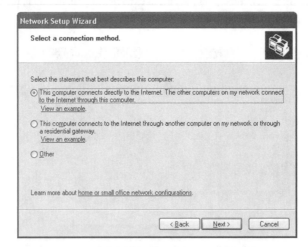

FIGURE 10.8 Specify how this computer connects to the Internet.

TIP

If all your computers connect to the Internet through a router connected to your cable or DSL box, treat each one as if it connected directly to the Internet.

⑤ If you chose Other in step 4, additional choices appear. Click the one you want and then click Next.
⑥ If you have more than one network adapter in your PC—for example, one for your Internet connection and one for your home network—you will be asked which card is for the Internet. Select it and then click Next.
⑦ Enter a name and description for the computer. These will appear when the other computers are browsing the network to find this one. See Figure 10.9. Then click Next.

CAUTION

If you already have a cable or DSL internet connection running on the computer, don't change the computer's name. Some services require your computer name to be a specific string of characters and letters, and if you change it, your Internet connection might not work anymore.

⑧ Specify a workgroup name, or leave the default MSHOME. You can use any name, but all the computers must use the same workgroup name. Using a different name than the default provides for slightly better security. Then click Next.

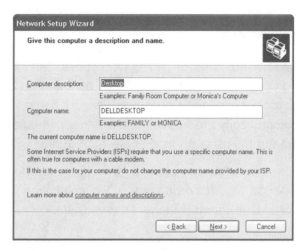

FIGURE 10.9 Enter the computer description and name.

⑨ If you are prompted to create a setup disk for other computers, do so if you have non-Windows-XP computers on your network; otherwise, skip this because you can run this wizard on the other PCs.

> **NOTE**
>
> The resulting floppy disk from step 9 can be taken to the other PCs in your home network and run there to set them up for networking. It's easy—you just follow the prompts.

⑩ Check the settings to confirm, and then click Next to apply them.
⑪ Wait for Windows to apply the new settings, then click Finish.
⑫ When prompted to restart your PC, click Yes to do so. When Windows restarts, this computer will be ready to participate in the network.

Now do the same thing on all the other PCs that will be part of the network. If they're all Windows XP computers—great. If not, use the Setup disk you created in step 9.

Working with a Network in Windows

Now that all your computers are physically networked and they are all set up for the same workgroup in Windows, you're ready to start sharing resources! The two main types of resources you can share are folders (and the files within them) and printers.

Sharing a Folder

Each Windows XP computer has a separate My Documents folder for each user account, plus a Shared Documents folder that all user accounts on that PC can access. When you set up a PC for networking through the Network Setup Wizard, this Shared Documents folder is automatically made available to other computers on your network. It is shared not only among the users on that single PC, but also within your network.

If you want to share some files, you can place them in that shared folder. The path to the Shared Documents folder on your hard disk is C:\Documents and Settings\All Users\Documents\Shared Documents, but there's an easier way to access it:

❶ Choose Start > My Documents.

❷ In the Other Places pane (to the left), click Shared Documents. To share a file or folder, move or copy it into this Shared Documents folder. You can also share other folders on your PC, and even entire drives (although that's not usually a good idea because of the security risk). To share another folder:

    a.   Open My Computer.

    b.   Find and select the icon for the folder you want to share. (Don't open the folder.)

    c.   Right-click the folder and choose Sharing and Security.

    d.   Mark the Share This Folder on the Network checkbox on the Sharing tab. See Figure 10.10.

❸ Enter a share name for the folder. By default it's the same name as the folder name, but you can change it if you like.

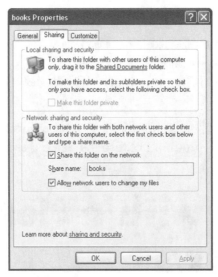

FIGURE 10.10 Sharing a folder.

④ (Optional) If you don't want others to be able to change the contents, clear the Allow Network Users to Change My Files checkbox.

⑤ Click OK.

Now the shared folder will appear when others are browsing the network.

Using a Shared Folder

You can browse the shared folders on other PCs in your network almost as easily as you can the folder on your own PC. Here's how:

① Choose Start > My Network Places.

② If a shortcut for the folder you want to browse appears, double-click it. By default, shortcuts to the Shared Documents folders of all other PCs in your workgroup appear, including your own. Figure 10.11 shows many shortcuts to shared folders on a network.

FIGURE 10.11 Browsing shared folders in My Network Places.

If a shortcut did not appear for the folder you wanted to browse on another PC, do the following to look for it:

① In the Network Tasks pane of the My Network Places window, click View Workgroup Computers.

② Icons for each of the computers in the workgroup appear. Double-click the one you want to browse.

From there it's just like browsing folders on your own computer. Only the folders that have been shared on that computer will appear.

TIP

From the My Network Places window, click Add a Network Place to set up a new shortcut. Then drag the shortcut to your desktop for quick access to it anytime.

Sharing a Printer

Sharing a printer is much like sharing a folder. You simply turn on its sharing options, as follows:

1 From the Control Panel (Classic View), double-click Printers and Faxes (or choose Start > Printers and Faxes if that command is available).

2 Right-click the printer icon and choose Sharing.

3 On the Sharing tab, click Share This Printer. See Figure 10.12.

4 (Optional) Change the name in the Share Name box to something descriptive.

5 Click OK.

FIGURE 10.12 Sharing a printer.

Using a Shared Printer

To use a shared printer, run the Add Printer Wizard and specify a network printer. You may need the setup disk that came with the printer, especially if the PC that will be accessing the shared printer has a different version of Windows than the one sharing it.

Here are the steps for configuring a PC to use a printer that some other PC has shared:

1 From the Control Panel (Classic View), double-click Printers and Faxes (or choose Start > Printers and Faxes if that command is available).

2 Click the Add a Printer hyperlink at the left. The Add Printer Wizard runs.

3 Click Next to begin.

4 Click the A Network Printer option button and click Next.

5 Leave Browse for a Printer marked and click Next.

6 A list of found printers on the network appears, as in Figure 10.13. (Yours will be different, of course.) Click the printer you want and click Next.

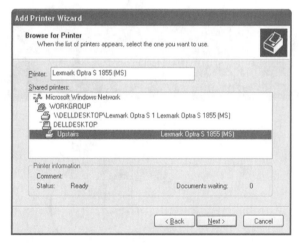

FIGURE 10.13 Choosing one of the shared printers to use.

7 Click Yes or No to use this as the default printer or not. Then click Next.

8 At the Completing screen, click Finish. Windows goes out to the network and downloads the driver for that printer from its local PC, and then it transfers the driver to your PC. If you have a different operating system, you might be prompted for the setup CD for the printer during this process.

You can now use the printer just as though it were connected directly to your own computer.

Sharing an Internet Connection

There are two ways to share an Internet connection. Each has its pros and cons.

If you have a broadband Internet connection (cable or DSL; satellite won't work for this) and a home network, you can add a *router* to your network (or use a router instead of an access point or hub), and the router will share the Internet connection for you, providing it to all your PCs automatically. Since each computer talks directly to the router, it doesn't rely on any other PC being up and running. There is also no burden placed on any one computer to handle sharing. The cons are that you have to buy a router, and you have to figure out how to configure it. (They usually come with good instructions, though.) In addition, it can be more difficult to configure file-sharing among PCs that connect through an Internet-access router. Figure 10.14 shows the connections.

Router: Like a hub, but "intelligent." A router is able to read the addresses on incoming and outgoing data and decide what to do with them. This makes it able to serve up a single Internet connection to multiple computers and intelligently direct the traffic to the computer that a particular message belongs to.

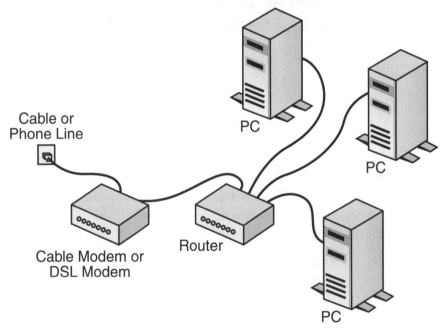

FIGURE 10.14 Connections for router-based connection sharing.

You can also share your Internet connection by having it come directly into one of your computers and then using the Internet Connection Sharing (ICS) feature in Windows XP to parse it out to the other computers on the network. See Figure 10.15. The pros are that it works with all kinds of Internet connections, including dial-up modems, and you don't have to buy any extra hardware. The cons are that the computer that has direct access must be on all the time, and if several computers are accessing the Internet at once, it can slow down the overall operation of the sharing computer. When you run the Network Setup Wizard (covered earlier in this chapter), it sets up Internet Connection Sharing automatically if you ask it to.

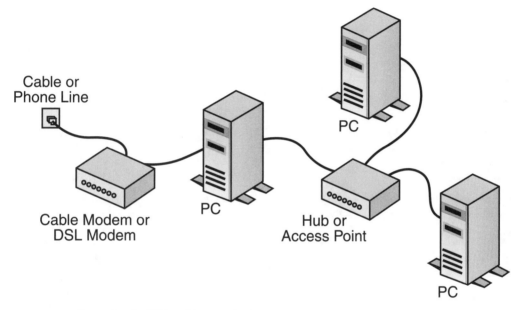

FIGURE 10.15 Connections for ICS-based Internet sharing.

10

11

Troubleshooting Common Errors

In this chapter:

- ◆ Solving startup problems
- ◆ Diagnosing problems with hardware devices
- ◆ Troubleshooting problems with applications
- ◆ Troubleshooting general Windows problems
- ◆ Reinstalling Windows

Your Dell PC will give you years of faithful service, but occasionally it needs your help in overcoming a software or hardware error. This chapter provides some tips for dealing with the most commonly occurring problems.

Solving Startup Problems

The scariest moment of all in computer ownership is when your PC won't start up. *What could be wrong with it?* Don't panic—just try to think. What have you done to the PC since the last time it started up? Then use that answer as a starting point for your troubleshooting.

TIP

Here's the king of all startup problems—and fortunately it's something simple. If you leave a floppy disk in your drive and restart, you'll get an error message, and Windows won't start. Pop out the floppy disk and try again.

Have You Installed Some New Hardware?

If you think the problem may be caused by new hardware you have recently added, remove it and try restarting the PC. (See Chapter 12, "Upgrading Your PC," for help adding new hardware.) If it starts up okay without the device, you've just identified the problem.

Of course, you still haven't figured out the main thing: Why does this piece of hardware cause a problem in Windows?

NOTE

Here's a strange little quirk: On some systems, having certain USB devices plugged into the PC as it is starting up will cause it to lock up. If you unplug the device, the PC boots normally; then you can plug the device back in afterward. Consult the Dell Support Web site (http://support.dell.com) to find out whether an update is available for your motherboard's BIOS (that is, its built-in software) that will solve the problem.

If a device is incorrectly installed or physically defective, it will probably just not work, and Windows won't even notice it. But there's a possibility that it could make Windows fail to boot.

However, in most cases it is not the hardware itself that causes Windows not to start, but the driver for it. When you install new hardware, Windows detects it and attempts to load a driver for it. Windows comes with a basic set of drivers, but you can also load a driver from the CD that came with the device. If you load the wrong driver for a device, it can cause the device not to work correctly (or at all), or—worst case—it could cause Windows to not be able to start up normally. See "Troubleshooting Application Problems," later in the chapter, for help with device driver issues.

> **Driver:** A file that translates instructions between Windows and a hardware device.

To solve such a problem, try shutting down the PC, removing the hardware, and restarting. If that doesn't help, start Windows in Safe Mode (see the following section "Starting Windows in Safe Mode") and remove the driver for the device (see "Removing or Disabling a Device Driver"). Still no luck? Try restoring a system restore snapshot, described later in the chapter.

Have You Installed a New Application?

Normally an application would not prevent Windows from starting up, but if the application is set to load automatically at startup, it could cause a problem. For example, suppose you install some shareware that is supposed to perform some useful background function, but it makes your PC lock up. When you reboot, that same program loads automatically at startup, and boom, you're locked up again, without any way of disabling the offending program.

The way out of such a problem is to start Windows in Safe Mode (see the following section) and then remove the application (see Chapter 4, "Adding, Removing, and Managing Programs"). If that doesn't work, restore a System Restore snapshot, as explained later in this chapter.

11

Starting Windows in Safe Mode

Safe Mode is a special troubleshooting mode for Windows XP. It loads the basic Windows XP interface but does not load anything non-essential. In most cases the item causing the problem is one of the non-essentials, so Windows is able to start up. Then you can fix the problem and reboot normally.

Safe Mode: A special startup mode that excludes most of the startup applications, drivers, and services in Windows XP so that you are able to get into the system for troubleshooting.

When your PC locks up instead of starting Windows normally, the next time you try to start it, you may see the Advanced Options menu, shown in Figure 11.1. If you do not, try pressing F8 as the PC is booting to display it.

TIP

It can be tricky to know exactly when to press F8, so I usually start pressing and releasing it at one-second intervals starting immediately after turning on the power until the menu appears. (You can't just hold down F8 because you'll get a Keyboard Stuck error.)

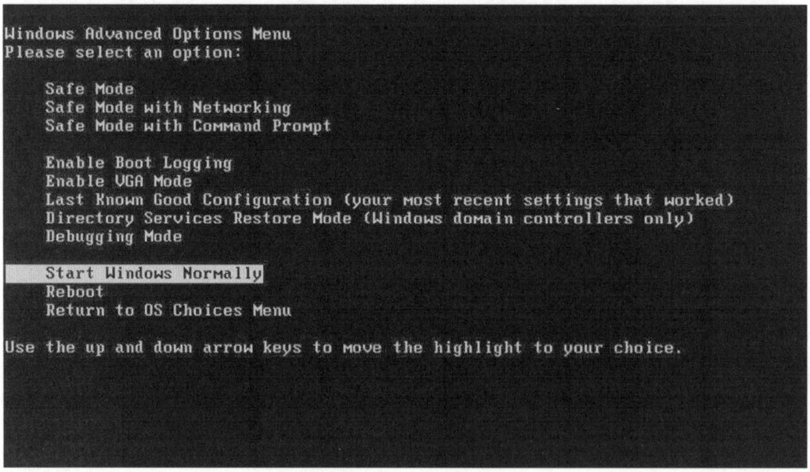

```
Windows Advanced Options Menu
Please select an option:

    Safe Mode
    Safe Mode with Networking
    Safe Mode with Command Prompt

    Enable Boot Logging
    Enable VGA Mode
    Last Known Good Configuration (your most recent settings that worked)
    Directory Services Restore Mode (Windows domain controllers only)
    Debugging Mode

    Start Windows Normally
    Reboot
    Return to OS Choices Menu

Use the up and down arrow keys to move the highlight to your choice.
```

FIGURE 11.1 Display this menu at startup by pressing F8.

From the Advanced Options menu, use the up/down arrow keys to select Safe Mode and press Enter. Windows will take longer than normal to start up and will be in a low-resolution video mode. Most non-essential devices don't work in Safe Mode, including your CD drives. From here you can remove an application that is causing a problem (see Chapter 4) or remove a device driver for some hardware that is causing a problem (see the following section).

Removing or Disabling a Device Driver

Usually when you remove a piece of hardware physically from your PC, Windows unloads its device driver automatically. However, this is not always the case, and the leftover driver can cause Windows problems if it is set to load when Windows starts up.

Here's how to remove a driver for a device that is causing a problem:

1. If feasible, turn off the PC and physically remove or disconnect the device. If you can't do this, skip it.
2. Turn the PC on and start in Safe Mode (see the previous section).
3. Open the Start menu, right-click My Computer, and choose Properties. The System Properties dialog box opens.
4. Click the Hardware tab, and click the Device Manager button.
5. In the Device Manager, if you do not see the device you want to remove, click the plus sign next to its category to find it. Then click the device to select it. See Figure 11.2.
6. If the hardware has been physically removed, uninstall the driver by doing any of the following:
   a. Right-click the device and choose Uninstall.
   b. Press the Delete key on the keyboard.
   c. Click the Uninstall button on the toolbar.
7. If you were not able to remove the hardware physically, disable the driver instead by doing one of the following:
   a. Right-click the device and choose Disable.
   b. Click the Disable button on the toolbar.
8. Close all open windows and restart. (Try to restart normally this time.)

11

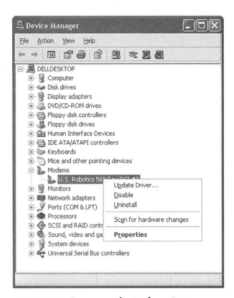

FIGURE 11.2 Remove a device from Device Manager by selecting it and pressing Delete.

What's the difference between Uninstall and Disable? Uninstall removes the driver and wipes the device from Windows' recollection. The next time you start your PC, if Windows detects that device, it will attempt to reinstall it. If you have removed the hardware physically, that won't be an issue, so it's okay to uninstall. Disable, on the other hand, lets Windows remember the device's physical presence but prevents its driver from loading. You would use this if you could not physically remove a device that was causing a problem.

Restoring a System Restore Point

Many software problems can be solved by restoring a system restore point. A *restore point* is a "snapshot" of your system files (including the Registry). Windows automatically takes one of these snapshots every day so that when problems occur you can revert back to the system state contained in that snapshot.

Restore point: A copy of the Windows Registry and a few other system files, stored at a particular date and time and made available through the System Restore utility.

It's important that you understand what a restore point does and doesn't offer. It is strictly a backup of the system state—it doesn't contain any application data. So for example, suppose that today I installed Microsoft Word and created a document called Today.doc with it. Then I used system restore to go back to yesterday's snapshot of the system. Windows would no longer think that Microsoft Word was installed, and it would not show up on the Start button's menu. However, the data file Today.doc would still exist, and if I poked around on the hard disk I could find most of the program files for Microsoft Word still there. System restore did not change the contents of the hard disk; it only changed the Windows Registry's perception of them.

Here's how to restore an ailing system that won't otherwise start due to some software problem:

1. Boot your PC in Safe Mode, as described in an earlier section.
2. Choose Start > All Programs > Accessories > System Tools > System Restore.
3. Choose Restore My Computer to an Earlier Time. A calendar appears, as in Figure 11.3. The days that have restore points available appear with bold numbers.
4. Click the desired day (yesterday, for example), and then click the desired restore point for that day (if more than one exists for that day).
5. Click Next and continue working through the Wizard as prompted. Your PC will restart, and afterward a box will appear, letting you know the restore was successful.

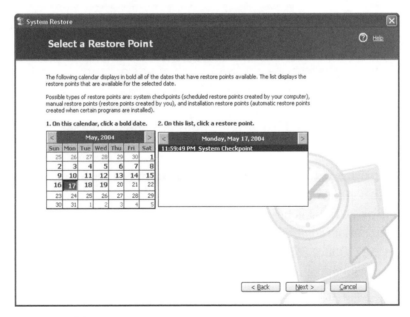

FIGURE 11.3 Select a restore point.

When system restore does a restore, it creates a restore point immediately beforehand. This makes all restorations reversible. Just go back in and reverse the last restoration if it made things worse.

TIP

The Last Known Good Configuration option on the Advanced Options menu (refer to Figure 11.1) is not quite the same thing as system restore, but similar. Whenever Windows boots successfully, it makes a backup of the Registry. This is an automatic, hidden backup set that you can't access with system restore. Choosing Last Known Good Configuration restores it. In contrast, the automatic backups that system restore makes are user accessible from within the System Restore utility.

Solving Other Hardware Problems

Now let's turn our attention to hardware problems that don't necessarily cause any problems with Windows startup.

Open up Device Manager, as you learned to do earlier in the chapter, and look for the device. Then troubleshoot as follows:

Device doesn't appear. A hardware failure has occurred when the device does not show up in Device Manager at all. Either the device is not installed correctly or it is defective. Remove and reinstall it, paying careful attention to the instructions that came with it. If needed, call the technical support phone number in the documentation.

Device appears as Other Device or Unknown Device or has an exclamation point next to its name. Windows sees this device, so the hardware is okay, but it is having a problem with the driver. The driver may be for the wrong model, it may not have been installed, or it may be outdated. Reinstall the driver from the CD that came with the device or (preferably) download and install a newer driver from the manufacturer's Web site.

Device appears fine in Device Manager but doesn't work. This is a software issue. Windows is ready to talk to the device, but for some reason the applications with which you are trying to access it don't see it correctly. Try reinstalling the application software that came with the device or reading its Help system to figure out how to make it work with your device. You might also check the Web site for the application to see if there are any known incompatibilities with certain brands and models of devices.

Troubleshooting Application Problems

Even though Windows XP itself is pretty stable, Microsoft has no control over the programmers who write other applications, so occasionally you may experience problems with applications not starting, terminating abruptly, or crashing the whole system. (Yes, sometimes even Microsoft applications crash, too!) Here are some troubleshooting tips:

Application won't install or won't run. Check the minimum system requirements on the application's box to make sure your system is up to the task. If that checks out okay, restart Windows XP and try again. If it's an older application, try the Setup program using the Program Compatibility Wizard. To do so, choose Start > All Programs > Accessories > Program Compatibility Wizard and follow the prompts. Still no good? Check the Web site for the application's manufacturer for troubleshooting tips.

Application runs but then locks up or terminates unexpectedly. This is probably a video or sound driver incompatibility with the software, especially if it's a game. Try updating the drivers for your video card and sound card from downloads from their respective manufacturer's Web sites. Also, visit the Web site for the application's manufacturer to learn about any possible workarounds.

11

> **TIP**
>
> Many games use DirectX to talk to your sound and video hardware. DirectX is a type of utility software (sort of like a driver) installed in Windows. Sometimes when you install a new game it will offer to install a new version of DirectX for you. This is a good idea because it will not overwrite a newer version. To test your PC's DirectX functionality, choose Start > Run. Type **dxdiag** and click OK. This opens a diagnostic utility especially for DirectX.

Sound or video in application is choppy. If the application involves a lot of video and sound and doesn't perform very well, it may simply be your computer's hardware not being quite up to the task. There's a difference between the minimum and the optimal hardware! Check the system requirements for the application and make sure your system has the right stuff. If not, consider an upgrade (see Chapter 12). Other things can cause poor performance besides hardware, though. Make sure all other applications have been closed before you run this one. Update the drivers for your sound and video hardware, and download any updates available for the application.

Troubleshooting General Windows Problems

Problems with Windows XP itself are fairly rare. It's a much more stable operating system than any previous version, with many more safety precautions built in, such that when one application crashes it usually does not bring the entire system down.

Though there are several errors that occasionally pop up, there is a single procedure for troubleshooting them: restart the PC. This flushes out whatever is in memory and reloads Windows afresh.

If you keep having frequent errors in Windows, and rebooting just isn't solving anything, see the following section.

Reinstalling Windows

To solve a particularly thorny problem with Windows itself—for example, frequent crashes or errors that won't go away no matter what you try—it may be necessary to reinstall Windows.

Before you take this drastic step, however, ask yourself the following questions:

◆ Does this problem occur more than with just one particular application?

◆ Does this problem occur more than with just one particular piece of hardware?

- Have you run a spyware/adware detection and removal application (see Chapter 6, "Ensuring Your Security and Privacy Online")?

- Have you installed, updated, and run an antivirus program (see Chapter 6)?

- Have you tried restoring the PC to an earlier configuration, before the problem started, with System Restore (covered earlier in this chapter)?

If you answered Yes to all the above, then you might benefit from reinstalling Windows.

The way you reinstall Windows depends on what kind of Windows XP CD you have: a system recovery CD from the PC maker, an upgrade version of Windows XP, or a full version of Windows XP.

Using a Recovery Disk

If you had Windows XP preinstalled on your PC, it likely came with a Reinstallation CD or System Recovery CD. Depending on the PC manufacturer, model, and age of your system, this CD might contain a full version of Windows XP, or it might contain a utility that will return your PC to its original factory state by wiping out the entire contents of your hard disk and reloading a backup of the original configuration.

CAUTION

Some System Recovery processes reset your PC back to the day you got it, in every way. *You will lose all your data*, as well as all your settings and applications. You can reinstall the applications later if you have the original disks for them, but make sure you back up all your data and settings beforehand. Read the documentation carefully that came with the CD to see what it does.

To use such a CD, insert it in your PC's floppy drive and allow your PC to start up from it. Then follow the directions onscreen. Your computer's documentation may have more information about it as well.

11

Reinstalling from a Windows XP CD

If you have a full version of Windows XP, you are covered no matter how you choose to reinstall Windows.

However, if you have the upgrade version, there's a potential snag. The upgrade version requires that you already have one of the eligible operating systems. It doesn't necessarily have to be installed on your PC, as long as you have the disk(s) for it.

Here are your choices:

◆ You can wipe out everything on your hard disk and reinstall a fresh copy of Windows from scratch. However, to do this with an upgrade Windows XP CD, you must also have the CD for an earlier Windows version available to insert as "proof of purchase" at some point during the setup process. With the full version, you won't need the earlier CD.

◆ You can reinstall the upgrade copy of Windows XP over the top of your current copy, with no "proof of purchase" needed for the upgrade version. This may fix some of the problems you have been experiencing, especially if any of them are due to missing or corrupted Windows system files. However, it's not a sure thing because the upgrade process is "considerate" of applications and utilities that are already installed and tends to leave them in place, and if one of them is causing the problem, the reinstallation will be of no help.

Whichever approach you want to take, insert the Windows XP CD in your CD drive and restart the PC. When you see the message Press Any Key to Boot from CD, do so, and the Windows setup process will begin. From there, just follow the prompts, indicating what you want.

12

Upgrading Your PC

In this chapter:

- ◆ Upgrading pros and cons
- ◆ Evaluating your PC's upgradeability
- ◆ Types of upgrades available
- ◆ Self-installation or professional?
- ◆ Tips for safely installing upgrades

sn't it amazing how quickly computer technology advances? And that's a good thing, because never before have new computers been so affordable. But that locomotive doesn't stop when you buy your PC—it keeps right on running. Therefore, whatever computer you buy today is going to seem out of date within a couple of years.

What's the solution—buy a new computer at that point or upgrade your old one? In this chapter I'll help you figure that out.

Upgrading versus Buying New

Unhappy with your current PC in some way? Is it too slow, or does it lack a particular feature or capability? You have three choices:

- ◆ Live with it.
- ◆ Upgrade it.
- ◆ Buy a whole new PC.

Living with it, obviously, is the most economical but least desirable choice. What about the other two choices?

Why Should You Upgrade?

Eventually you will need to buy a new PC. There will come a day when that old one breaks and won't be worth the cost to fix it, or when you throw up your hands in disgust because it is so slow or because it can't run the new application you just bought.

However, today is perhaps not that day. Upgrading can be the most cost-effective solution when your current PC is lacking in only one or two areas.

Advantages of upgrading include:

Lower short-term cost. Why replace the entire PC if only one item is broken or inadequate, or if there is only one new feature it lacks? You can save hundreds of dollars in the short term by buying only what you need.

Extended PC life. The longer you can put off buying a whole new PC, the more PC you will get for your money. Upgrading one or two items in an old PC can make living with it more pleasant for another year or so, and a year from now you will get a much faster CPU.

Addition of new features. You can add the latest capabilities to an existing PC fairly economically, such as a writeable DVD drive. Buying a whole new PC just to have one new feature would be overkill.

Why *Shouldn't* You Upgrade?

There are two sides to every decision, so in the interest of fairness, I will now try to talk you *out* of upgrading your computer.

New computers are inexpensive. New computers are a very good value these days. If you stick with your old monitor, you can have a decent-quality new PC for about $500. Not bad!

Buying a new computer is easy. Face it—upgrading is a hassle. You have to decide where the bottleneck is in your system's performance, select the right part, install it (or pay to have it installed), and then fret about whether it made any difference. With a new computer, you know you've got the good stuff.

Professional installation costs money. If you aren't up to the challenge of installing the upgrades yourself, expect to pay $50 or more to have someone else do it. That's $50 you could have put toward the price of a new PC.

Sharing is good. If you buy a new PC, you can give your old one to a deserving family member or friend or donate it to charity (and take a tax write-off).

New PCs are balanced. Think about water flowing through a narrow pipe. If you replace one section of the pipe with a really wide piece, will the water flow any faster? Probably not. Similarly, if you upgrade one part of an old PC, you have an old PC with one new part, and some other part will probably start being a bottleneck.

12

New PCs come with software. If you don't have the latest versions of Windows and Microsoft Office but you want them, you will be able to get them cheaper bundled with a new PC than you can buy them at retail.

New PCs come with warranties. New computers have at least a one-year warranty for the whole thing. If you buy new upgrade parts, they have their own warranties, but when an individually warranted part breaks you have to narrow down the problem to that part, ship it off to the company (at your own expense), and install the replacement. With a whole-system warranty, you can take the ailing PC to an authorized repair center and have them figure it out for you.

The Type of Upgrade Makes a Difference

Besides the overall pros and cons I've pointed out so far, there are also special considerations, depending on the type of upgrade. Here are some of the most common upgrades and my recommendation:

RAM. Adding RAM makes sense if your computer doesn't have much of it (for example, if it has 128MB or less) and if your PC is otherwise good-to-go. Having more RAM can boost your PC's performance somewhat, and it's fairly easy to install. The tricky part is making sure you buy the right kind. Consult the Dell Support Web site (http://support.dell.com) to look up your PC by its serial number or Express Service Code to find out what to buy.

CPU. Upgrading the CPU can be tricky, and I don't recommend it. Because most motherboards accept only a certain class of CPUs, you probably won't find a dramatically better CPU than the one you have that will work with your motherboard. It is also easy to ruin a CPU with electrostatic discharge (that is, static electricity) while handling it.

Motherboard. I don't recommend this upgrade because you will probably need new RAM and a new CPU to go with it, and by the time you pay for all that plus professional installation, you've paid almost as much as you would for a whole new computer.

Hard Disks. Adding a new hard disk can be a good upgrade, provided there is nothing else major wrong with your PC. On most systems you can add the new drive as a secondary drive, so you don't have to get rid of your original one. It's like adding a room addition to your house.

CD and DVD Drives. Adding CD or DVD drives (writeable or otherwise) can be a good upgrade, too. If all you want is the capability to create your own CDs or DVDs, and your PC is basically okay except for that, this makes a lot of sense.

Video Cards. Unless you are a serious gamer and are finding your current video card inadequate, there is little reason to upgrade the video card. You won't see a lot of performance improvement on most systems. It's not a difficult upgrade, though— you just pop out one circuit board and pop in another, like with the modem in Chapter 5, "Getting Started with the Internet."

Sound Cards. Same thing with the sound card as with the video card. It's an easy upgrade, but it won't improve system performance except perhaps with games that have complex sound systems.

External Devices. Just about anything external you can add or upgrade is a good thing because you can use it with any new computers you might buy in the future, so your upgrade money is not wasted. This could include printers, scanners, bar code readers, speakers, keyboard, mouse, and so on.

Evaluating Your PC's Upgradeability

Before you get too much further into your upgrade plans, take a look at your current hardware. (Hey, you did this in Chapter 1, "Choosing and Setting Up a Computer," so now you've come full circle.) This time, however, you're looking at it in terms of open slots, ports, and bays to determine what upgrade parts you can add.

External Upgrades

External upgrades require free ports on the back (or front) of the PC to which to connect. Check the specifications for the upgrade device you plan to buy to see what type of port it needs. Figure 12.1 points out some of the most common ports on the back of a typical PC.

Notice in Figure 12.1 that the FireWire ports have been added via a circuit board inserted in the PC (as described in the next section); they are not built in like the rest of

12

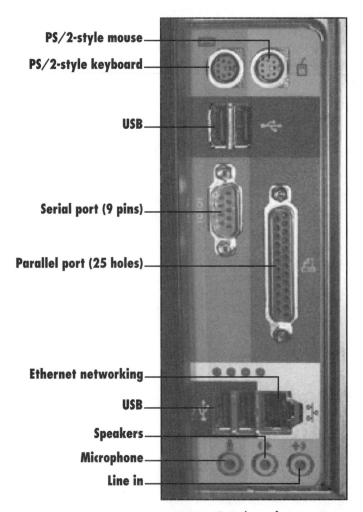

PS/2-style mouse
PS/2-style keyboard

USB

Serial port (9 pins)

Parallel port (25 holes)

Ethernet networking

USB

Speakers

Microphone

Line in

FIGURE 12.1 Typical ports for connecting external components.

the ports in this system. Some systems do have a FireWire port built in, but this one does not. Their presence in this figure highlights an important point—that you can usually add whatever ports you need via expansion boards.

Circuit Board Additions

Circuit boards are inserted into slots in the motherboard. If you're replacing one video or sound card with another, this is no problem—out with the old, in with the new. But if you're adding without subtracting, you'll need a free slot.

Peripheral Connection Interface (PCI) is the common all-purpose slot type for upgrades. These are the white slots in the motherboard, the same type you saw in Chapter 5 when we were installing a modem. Most motherboards have at least three of them, but one or more might already be taken. See Figure 12.2.

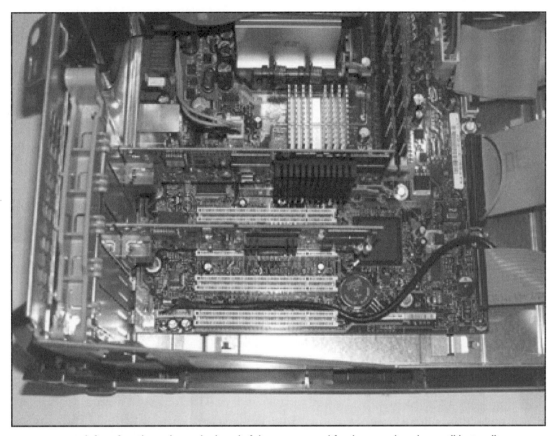

FIGURE 12.2 Look for a free slot in the motherboard of the type required for the circuit board you will be installing.

Some motherboards might have other slots as well. For example, there might be a brown or bright green AGP slot (Accelerated Graphics Port, for video cards only). In an older PC there might also be one or more black ISA slots (an older type of slot, mostly obsolete now).

12

Disk Drive Additions

If you will be replacing an existing disk drive—no worries. But if you're adding one, you must look inside the PC's case and make sure several things are present:

◆ **A free power supply connector.** These are the plastic plugs with four wires that come out of the power supply. Floppy drives require the small ones (on the left in Figure 12.3); all other drives require the large ones (on the right).

FIGURE 12.3 Power connectors for drives inside the PC.

◆ **An empty externally accessible drive bay.** All drives that use removable disks must be placed in bays that can be accessed from outside the PC. Floppy drives and ZIP drives can use the small bays; all CD and DVD drives must use the larger ones. Look for blank pop-out panels on the front of your PC for free externally accessible bays.

◆ **An empty internally accessible drive bay.** Hard disks do not need externally accessible bays, but they do need bays. The small ones will do. If all you have free are large ones, you can get brackets that will allow a small drive to be housed in a large bay.

✦ **A free EIDE connector.** All drive types except floppies use the EIDE interface on the motherboard. (There are other interfaces for drives, such as Serial ATA and SCSI, but they aren't common in today's consumer-level PC systems.) They connect to the motherboard using ribbon cables. There are two EIDE connectors on the motherboard, and each can support two drives, so you can have a total of four EIDE drives in the system. As long as you have fewer than four, you're okay adding one. If you already have four, you would need to add a circuit board (see the previous section) with an additional EIDE connector on it.

CAUTION

As you are poking around in the PC, try not to touch anything. It's easy to damage components with static electricity. For this reason, many people wear special antistatic wrist straps or stand on antistatic mats when they work on computers.

Do You Want Professional Installation?

At this point perhaps you are thinking, "There's no way I can do this myself!" Installing upgrades in a PC can be intimidating for the beginner. Fortunately, help is available. You're not alone.

For starters, most upgrade components come with clear instructions for their installation, including pictures. If you are a moderately good at following directions (for example, if you can put together pre-fab furniture), you should be able to install your own upgrades.

There are entire books written on the subject of upgrading a computer, with step-by-step instructions and pictures. While these are not specific to your model of computer or to the upgrade model you bought, they can be of tremendous help in familiarizing you with the upgrade process in general, so you can make intelligent decisions. The manual that came with your PC might also have some instructions and pictures.

Finally, there are service departments at local computer stores where friendly and knowledgeable technicians will install the upgrades for you.

12

I don't want to discourage you from self-installing if you feel up to it, but if you're having any anxiety at all about it, consider professional installation, for these reasons:

◆ **No worries about buying incompatible parts.** If you opt for professional installation, you don't have to go through that whole process of figuring out what components you have, what slots are available, and so on. Just take your PC in and say "I want more memory," or "I want a DVD burner," and the technicians there will identify and install the right stuff.

◆ **No worries about parts being incorrectly installed.** If you install it yourself and it doesn't work, will you be able to tell whether it is defective or whether you simply did it wrong? Professional technicians install hundreds of upgrades a week. They know how this stuff works.

◆ **No worries about defective parts.** If you install it yourself and the part is defective, you must package it back up and return it for a refund/exchange. On the other hand, if the technician performing your upgrade determines that a part is defective, he will simply replace it from stock.

For a lot of people, all of those "no worries" are well worth the money paid for professional services.

Tips for Safe Self-Installation

If you have decided to do your own upgrading, you'll want to observe some basic safety precautions. Keep these in mind as you follow the specific step-by-step instructions that come with the upgrade components you purchase.

Avoiding Damage from Static Electricity

Static electricity (also called electrostatic discharge, or ESD) is deadly to computer components, even small amounts, so whenever you are working inside a PC, wear rubber-soled shoes, wear natural fabrics, and work in a room with high humidity. All these things prevent high levels of static charge from building up in your body.

Damage occurs to components when you touch something that has a lower electrical charge than your body does. To minimize the damage, minimize the differences in the charges. One way is to touch the PC's metal frame frequently as you work. Any excess charge flows from your body to the metal frame, so it's not available to harm any more sensitive pieces that you might subsequently touch.

> **NOTE**
>
> How much static electricity does it take to damage a computer component? *Very, very little.* Humans notice it when it gets to be 3,000 volts or so, but as little as one volt can damage a component. When shocked, a component might stop working immediately or it might simply be weakened so that it fails later.

For extra peace of mind about avoiding ESD, wear an antistatic wrist strap with one end attached to the PC's metal frame and the other end to your wrist. This keeps the electrical charges equalized as you work. They are not very expensive ($10 or so), and most computer stores carry them. See Figure 12.4.

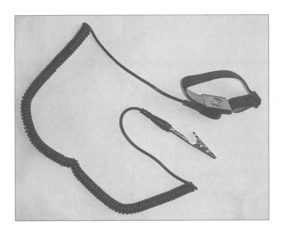

FIGURE 12.4 An antistatic wrist strap.

Most circuit boards and drives come in special antistatic plastic bags. Keep them in the bags until you are ready to install them. When you do remove one from its bag, *don't* set it on top of the bag.

Don't handle a circuit board any more than necessary, and when you do touch it, hold it only by its edges. This is not only to avoid physically bending parts on the board, but also to avoid passing any electrical charges to them.

12

Avoiding Harm to Yourself

PCs are not particularly hazardous to humans, but they're not foolproof. Here are some tips for keeping yourself safe when installing PC upgrades:

- ◆ Unplug the PC before removing its cover. Just turning it off is not enough. Some technicians leave a computer plugged in while working on it to keep it grounded and avoid static electricity build-up, but this is a bad idea, especially on modern systems where the motherboard continues to get power even when the PC is off.

- ◆ Don't disassemble a computer's power supply (the big metal box inside with the colored wires coming out of it). If it's defective, replace it.

- ◆ Don't remove the cover on a CRT monitor or stick anything into its vents. CRT monitors (the big boxy type) have a large capacitor inside that can store over 30,000 volts even when the PC has been unplugged for several weeks.

- ◆ Don't wear jewelry made of metal that conducts electricity as you work on your PC.

- ◆ Don't wear jewelry that dangles, such as hoop earrings or a necklace; it could get caught on something.

- ◆ Be careful not to stab or scratch yourself on any sharp metal pieces that stick out of circuit boards.

- ◆ Avoid picking up a PC by its frame when the cover is off, because some of the bars on the case might not be well secured and could come off.

- ◆ Because some PCs cases have sharp metal edges inside them, use care when putting a hand down inside a case.

- ◆ Do not attempt to thwart built-in safeguards for any components.

- ◆ Do not leave circuit boards lying on the floor where someone could step on them.

In Conclusion...

Congratulations on making it through the book! You might have started out with zero experience in Chapter 1, but you now have the skills you need to use and maintain your computer with confidence. You can install and remove programs, manage files, make CDs and DVDs, work with scanners and digital cameras, connect to the Internet, and much more! And now that you have completed this chapter, you also know how to select and evaluate upgrades for your PC and how to keep safe if you decide to install them yourself.

For more information about PC use and care, check the Dell Training and Certification Web site at http://LearnDell.com to see what classes and other resources are currently being offered.

12

Glossary

Access point: A wireless network hub. See *hub.*

Adware: Software designed to display ads on your computer.

Application: Software that works with the operating system to enable you to do something useful, such as write a letter or balance a checkbook. Examples include word processors, spreadsheets, databases, and games.

Autorun: A Windows feature that enables a program on a CD-ROM to run automatically when you insert the CD.

Broadband: A network connection that is capable of carrying many bits of data simultaneously, resulting in fast overall throughput.

CD-ROM drive: A regular CD drive. It plays CDs but not DVDs, and it does not write to either CDs or DVDs.

CD-RW drive: A drive that reads CDs and writes to CD-R (write-once) and CD-RW (write multiple times) discs.

Central Processing Unit (CPU): A microchip that serves as the "brain" of the computer, processing most of the mathematical operations that make it function.

Click: To move the mouse so its pointer touches an item onscreen and then press and release the left mouse button once.

Client: A computer that uses the services provided on a network.

Codec: A software utility that decodes the data from a compressed audio or video file. Different file formats compress and encode data in different ways, so each player must have a codec for each format it supports.

Control Panel: An area of Windows from which you can access the options for various types of hardware and software. To display it, click the Start button and then click Control Panel.

Cookies: Plain text identifier files that certain Web pages place on your hard disk so that they can identify you on future visits and maintain your settings (such as a shopping cart or wish list).

CRT: Stands for cathode ray tube. This is the traditional "box" kind of monitor that has been used ever since PCs were first developed. They are bulky and heavy but cheap.

Desktop: The onscreen background on which various items can be placed. Can also refer to the Windows XP operating environment in general.

Dialog box: A window that offers settings to choose from, plus an OK button to accept the settings and a Cancel button to reject the changes.

Dial-up: A connection between computers that involves a modem and a telephone line. Dial-up connections must be established and disconnected by the user as they are needed; they are not always on.

Digitize: To convert to digital (computer) format.

Disk: A flat circular platter that spins on a central axis and stores data on its surface.

Double-click: To press and release the left mouse button quickly twice in succession.

Download: To transfer a file from someone else's computer to your own. See *upload*.

Drag: To press and hold the left mouse button down and then move the mouse.

Drive: A mechanical unit that reads and writes data on a disk or on magnetic tape. It typically includes a motor that drives the spindle that turns the disk, a read/write head on a movable arm, and a disk intake and ejection system.

Driver: A file that translates instructions between Windows and a hardware device.

DVD±R drive: A drive that reads DVDs and writes them in both DVD+R and DVD-R format.

ESD: Electrostatic discharge, or static electricity. It can harm the sensitive electronics inside a computer.

Ethernet: A common network technology used for most home and business networks.

File extension: The file type identifier code following the period in the file's name.

Firewall: A program or device that prevents other users on the Internet from browsing or altering the contents of your hard drive through your Internet connection.

Fragmented: Not stored in one contiguous location.

Hard disk: A sealed set of metal platters for storing data. The hard disk is typically the primary storage device for the operating system and any installed applications, as well as the data files you create using those applications.

Hardware: Physical computer equipment such as drives, circuit board, cases, and chips.

Home page: The Web page that the browser software is configured to begin with each time you start it. Can also refer to the top-level page of a multipage Web site.

G

Hub: A box that serves as a physical gathering point for network cables in a network workgroup.

Hyperlink: A bit of text or a graphic that, when clicked, opens a certain Web page, document, or e-mail window.

Icon: A small picture, usually with words underneath it, representing a file, folder, or application.

Input device: A device that helps you get data into the computer.

Insertion point: A vertical flashing cursor that shows where the text you enter will be placed.

Internet: A worldwide public network of interconnected computers.

LCD: Liquid crystal display. This is the flat kind of monitor, shown in Figure 1.9. They are thin and lightweight and produce beautiful images. However, they are more expensive than CRTs, especially for large sizes.

Logical error: An error on a disk that is caused by a filing problem rather than a physical defect. Compare to *physical error*.

Mail server: A computer that serves as a post office for your e-mail. It stores your incoming e-mail until you pick it up, and it forwards your outgoing e-mail to the recipient.

MIDI: Musical Instrument Digital Interface, an interface for connecting electronic musical instruments to a computer.

Modem: Short for modulator-demodulator. A device that translates digital data from a computer into audio signals for transmission over phone lines and then back again at the other end.

Motherboard: A big circuit board that serves as a central gathering point inside a PC. The RAM and CPU are mounted on it, and most of the other inside components connect to it also.

Network adapter: A device that helps the PC send data to and from the network. It is sometimes called a network interface card (NIC), although these days there are other types besides cards, such as circuit boards.

Notification area: Icons for programs that are running in the background appear here. You might have an icon here for your antivirus program, for example.

OCR: Optical character recognition, a software feature that enables pages of scanned text to be converted into characters of text that can be edited in a text editor.

Operating system: The software that starts up your PC and keeps it running. It enables you to manage your data files and communicate with input and output devices. Microsoft Windows XP is the most popular operating system today.

Output device: A device that displays data that's coming out of the computer.

PC: Personal computer, a computer designed for one person to use at a time. A personal computer can run any of a variety of operating systems, but the term PC is most often associated with a computer running Microsoft Windows.

PCI: Peripheral Connect Interface, a high-speed, general-purpose slot on the motherboard for adding circuit boards that expand the PC's capabilities.

Peer to peer: A type of network in which there is no server to manage the network, so each of the client computers shares equally in the burden of maintaining the network.

Physical error: A physical defect on the disk surface that causes whatever is stored in that spot to be unreadable.

Pin: To attach a shortcut for a program to the top-left area of the Start menu.

Pixel: A colored dot on the display.

Point: To move the mouse so that the pointer arrow's tip touches a certain object onscreen.

Power supply: The component inside the PC that converts the incoming 110 volt AC current from the wall outlet to power that the PC can use (DC current between +2 and +12 volts).

Program Compatibility Wizard: A feature that helps you set up Windows XP to run software designed for earlier Windows versions.

Protocol: A language that a network component uses to speak to other components. The most popular one is TCP/IP, which is also the protocol used on the Internet.

RAM: Random access memory, a set of microchips that work together to create a temporary holding area for data as the computer is operating.

Recycle Bin: The temporary storage area that holds deleted files. You can retrieve files from here before they are permanently deleted.

Refresh rate: The rate at which the pixels on the display are refreshed.

G

Registry: The configuration file that tells Windows about your hardware, software, and system settings. Each time Windows starts, it reads and applies these settings.

Restore point: A copy of the Windows Registry and a few other system files, stored at a particular date and time and made available through the System Restore utility.

Right-click: To press and release the right mouse button once.

Right-drag: To press and hold down the right mouse button and then move the mouse.

Router: Like a hub, but "intelligent." A router is able to read the addresses on incoming and outgoing data and decide what to do with it. This makes it able to serve up a single Internet connection to multiple computers and intelligently direct the traffic to the computer that a particular message belongs to.

Safe Mode: A special startup mode that excludes most of the startup applications, drivers, and services in Windows XP so that you are able to get into the system for troubleshooting.

Scan resolution: The number of pixels (dots) per inch the original image will be segmented into when scanned. A higher dots per inch (dpi) results in a larger file size but results in a better quality photo when printed.

Server: A computer that provides services to other computers on a network rather than doing anything directly for a human user.

Shortcut: An icon that serves as a pointer to a file or folder. A single file can have many shortcuts to it in different locations, making access to it more convenient.

Software: Programming instructions or data that can be run or displayed on a computer.

Spam: Computer slang for junk e-mail. The name comes from a Monty Python comedy sketch where the word spam is repeated over and over, drowning out everything else.

Spyware: A type of software that runs in the background on a PC and sends information back to its creator through a network or Internet connection.

Streaming: An audio or video clip that plays directly from the Internet, and which you can't store on your PC for later use; others are fully downloadable.

Terminal adapter: The DSL equivalent of a modem. It is not really a modem because it is all digital—it does not convert between sound and data. Many people call it a DSL modem, however.

Theme: A collection of appearance settings saved under a common name.

Trojan horse: A program that pretends to do something useful but actually harms your computer or opens up a security hole that someone can use to view your private files or do other bad things when you are not noticing.

Upload: To transfer a file from your computer to someone else's. See *download*.

URL: Uniform resource locator. The address of a Web page or other content on the Internet.

Virus: A bit of code that attaches itself to an executable file (that is, a program file). When you run that program, the virus is copied into RAM and can spread itself to other programs you run. Many viruses can also copy themselves to the startup area of a disk so that they load into memory whenever you start the computer using that disk.

Window: An onscreen box containing an application, a set of options from which to choose, or a listing of files and folders.

Worm: A program that spreads itself via e-mail or the Web. Some of them attach themselves to all your outgoing e-mail; others go so far as to mail themselves to everyone in your e-mail address book.

G

Index

A